W9-BKC-623

An Angel
by Your Side

Publications International, Ltd.

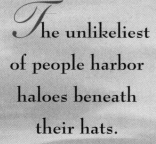

The unlikeliest of people harbor haloes beneath their hats.

Introduction written by Margaret Anne Huffman.

Contributing writers: Burky Achilles: 278; Joanne Baily Baxter: 219; Dianne Benton: 135; Renie Szilak Burghardt: 228; Wyn Esselborn: 143; Susan Fahncke: 259; Pat Gilbers: 174; Amber Gregory: 33; Carole Hall: 221; Bonnie Compton Hanson: 55, 57, 167; Shelia S. Hudson: 62; Margaret Anne Huffman: 66, 130, 161, 170, 180, 212, 232, 244; Ellen Javernick: 21, 27, 78, 106, 115, 126, 149, 177, 249; Marie Jones: 16, 24, 31, 40, 92, 110, 139, 145; Karen Leet: 10, 46, 59, 74, 83, 118, 286; Susie Levan as told to M.L. Pessoa: 155; Irene Messina: 238; Barbara Morrow: 49, 52, 122, 124; Kathleen Muldoon: 256; Lillian S. Murphy: 153; Carol McAdoo Rehme: 14, 88, 102, 192, 263, 267, 269, 273, 275, 282; Susan Sage: 200; LeAnn Thieman: 197; Diana Thrift: 69, 96, 205; Elizabeth Toole: 185; Ted Wagner: 203.

Acknowledgments:

Publications International, Ltd., has made every effort to locate the owners of all copyrighted material to obtain permission to use the selections that appear in this book. Any errors or omissions are unintentional; corrections, if necessary, will be made in future editions.

Scripture taken from the New Revised Standard Version of the Bible, copyright © 1989, by the Division of Christian Education of the National Council of the Churches of Christ in the United States of America, and are used by permission. All rights reserved.

Picture credits:

Front cover (bottom left) & back cover (top left): **Orion Press/Black Sheep Stock Photography.**

Art Resource: Fine Art Photographic Library, London: 203, 214; Scala: 87; **The Crosiers:** 3, 5, 25, 50, 63, 114, 171, 188, 198, 230, 248, 268; **FPG International:** Paul & Linda Marie Ambrose: 17, 284; Dennie Cody: 72, 246; David Doody: 34; Farrell Grehan: 15; Peter Gridley: 118; Telegraph Colour Library: 146; VCG: 112; **Ron Sanford/International Stock:** 116; SuperStock: 11, 38, 41, 56, 93, 101, 121, 190, 223, 254; John Bunker: 12; 270, 273; Cappella Baglioni, Church of Saint Maria Maggiore, Spello, Italy: 45; Christie's Images: 224, 227; Maurice Faulk: 184, 219; Galleria Dell' Academia, Florence/Bridgeman Art Library, London: 236; The Grand Design: 89, 209; Mauro Magliani/San Pietro, Belluno, Italy: 144; Roy Miles Gallery, London/Bridgeman Art Library, London: 281; Museo Civico, Udine, Italy/ET Archive, London: 195; Museo Diocesano, Cortona, Italy: 64; Newberry Library, Chicago: 160; Palazzo Ducale, Mantua, Italy: 9; Palazzo Medici-Riccardi, Florence, Italy/Bridgeman Art Library, London: 108; Pinacoteca, Volterra, Italy: 148; Private Collection/Bridgeman Art Library, London: 262; Private Collection/Diana Ong: 84; Private Collection/Arnold Rice: 138.

Copyright © 2002 Publications International, Ltd. All rights reserved. This book may not be reproduced or quoted in whole or in part by any means whatsoever without written permission from:

Louis Weber, CEO
Publications International, Ltd.
7373 North Cicero Avenue
Lincolnwood, Illinois 60712

Permission is never granted for commercial purposes.

Manufactured in China.

8 7 6 5 4 3 2 1

ISBN: 0-7853-4893-X

Library of Congress Catalog Card Number: 00-109684

Contents

Angels Watching Over Us

Then an angel of the Lord stood before them.
Luke 2:9

"*All night, all day, angels watchin' over me, my lord,*" proclaims the familiar spiritual. Angels watching over us—what a comforting thought.

Many people believe that angels watch over us. More than half of all adults, according to researchers, believe in angels. One person in seven claims to have had a personal experience with an angel. There's a reason why 75 percent of all Christmas trees are adorned with angels. We need our angels.

As the stories contained in the following pages of *An Angel by Your Side* will remind you, angels are always ready to assist us. When we need help, one of God's angels appears in the midst of our lives.

This beautiful book brings us into companionship with God through stories by people who have been hovered over, protected, and cared for by angels. There is comfort in knowing that God guards each of us personally and visits us one-on-one. Angels are as trustworthy as day following night.

Angels are as close as our outstretched hands. They reach for us as hands of support beneath our elbows, as hands tending us in illness and darkest despair, as hands holding ours when we are afraid, and as hands patting our shoulders in encouragement. Whatever the circumstances, we get the message: God cares.

Why are angels so important to us?

The original Hebrew word for angel is "messenger." And message carriers they are, whether they be divine or human.

In ancient days there were no telephones, fax machines, or e-mail. The only way to communicate was to go wherever the person was or to send a messenger. Most of the world's business in ancient times was taken care of by messengers. Ancient people saw these messengers as having the same power or acting with power on behalf of the rulers who sent them. So when an angel of God visits earth, it announces the presence of God through the messenger.

Angels can also remind us that God has a task for us to do. When Gabriel came to Mary, he said, "Do not be afraid, Mary, for you have found favor with God." The angel told Mary of the comfort and the power of God's presence. And then Gabriel went on to tell her that she would give birth to Jesus. The gifts of angels are comfort, presence, and power in the midst of fear.

We most often think of angels at Christmastime. Christmas is about the unexpected and unbelievable. The first surprise is that God sent his son, who became one of us and joined us in this life. The second surprise of Christmas is that God is still with us today—through the communication of angels all around us.

But the message that angels carry is without season. It is simply this: *We are not alone.*

Are angels a dream, a wish? Are they merely a marketing gimmick, a cute collectible to put on a shelf and gather dust?

No, they are a real presence in the lives they enter.

Secure in this knowledge, we collect angel paraphernalia, wear angel jewelry, sing angel carols, dress our children like angels at Christmas, and show appreciation by saying, with gratitude, "You're such an angel."

Life is full of moments that only you and your angel share.

We pore over books, poems, and Scripture verses, and we delight in movies and television shows about angels. We search the heavens and corners of our lives, hoping they will be there, for we believe the promise that God is with us. Not only do angels carry messages of God's love, some of them are guardians, interceding, nudging, prompting...even becoming involved in our lives to protect and defend us against danger and injury.

When we are fortunate enough to be touched by an angel, we welcome them as they comfort us, intervene for us, and accompany us. Uncertain how they'll appear, we are nevertheless assured that they will. When they do, we are touched forever by the generous spirit of God's love.

We should not doubt that angels come to us, even though it is amazing and awesome that they do. Those who have experienced a wondrous visitation by an angel urge others to open our minds to God's limitless presence. Read between the lines of the following inspired and inspiring pages. You will find reassurance that, yes, angels are here, tending and overseeing us, taking care of us.

Literature, both secular and religious, ancient and present-day, carries many stories detailing the marvelous intervening work done by these special messengers. Readers of *An Angel by Your Side* are invited into places where an interested and ever-present God is revealed through the work and caring of his angels—wherever *we* are. For there is *no* situation that is beyond God's interest and involvement. These stories, anecdotes, poems, and sayings tell just how angels amazingly appear and how our lives are forever changed in the encounter.

In this book you will read of loving angels who let us know how important and cared for we are. You'll find a touching story of an unmarried teenage mother who now, many years later, counsels and cares for teenagers in the same situation.

You'll also see guiding angels who have helped give someone's life directon—read of a golf coach's lessons that affect his golf team long after their college years, and even after his own death. There are stories of the angels who are all around us—read of a small child who helps an overweight woman see herself as beautiful, of a neighborhood that helps a family through a medical crisis with their youngest child, of a Red Cross volunteer and a police office who search through rubble created by a tornado to find a small child's best friend—her treasured doll.

You'll also read stories of messenger angels who warn people in times of danger, of faithful angels who stand ready to help during times of uncertainty, of guardian angels who watch over and protect, of healing angels who work on both body and soul, and of comforting angels who console and give solace. As we read, we find that God is always there, ready to send an interceding presence.

Turning the pages of *An Angel by Your Side*, you'll discover that as we accept the possibility of angels watching over us, we can trust God more each day. With eyes open we are more receptive to the presence of heavenly messengers

A richly filled book, *An Angel by Your Side* is a personal inspirational companion to keep on a bedside table or in a briefcase, as well as a thoughtful gift to give to a friend who needs a reminder and reassurance of God's presence and companionship.

Beautiful artwork and illustrations offer further illumination, as do uplifting thoughts throughout. As we read, we are reminded of the joy and security that comes from companionship with a God who has sent loving messengers to surround us in every event of our lives.

How comforting to know that the God of Love is nearby—as close as angel wings beating gently upon our hearts.

Angels All Around

Recognizing the presence of angels around you can feel like walking from the shadows into the warmth of sunshine. Suddenly, you feel the nourishment that comes from someone taking the time to look out just for you and you alone.

Stranger on the Street

Oh, I felt good about myself. I was so pleased with what a nice, kind, thoughtful person I was. I'd just spent hours laboring away at volunteer tasks, giving my time to help others. I'd helped take care of patients in a nursing home, reading letters to them, chatting with them. My head was full of self-congratulation. I was feeling incredibly virtuous, wonderfully delighted with myself, absolutely superior to lesser folk who were too selfish and preoccupied to reach out to those in need.

Fully absorbed in myself and what a great person I'd become, I scarcely noticed the grubby stranger heading my way. He aimed straight at me as if I were the only person out on the streets that day. When I suddenly noticed him, I braced myself. Uh oh. I could see his filthy clothes, torn and stained. Clearly he'd spent months on the streets, perhaps living in doorways or beneath bridges, huddled in boxes or wrapped in newspapers for warmth.

I dreaded the confrontation. Being approached by homeless people made me feel immensely uncomfortable. I knew I should try to help but felt unable to do anything. If I gave someone cash, it might be used badly. And what else could I do? Besides, I didn't have much money anyway. Finances were tight. Every penny counted. In fact, I was walking home to save bus fare. With the coins I'd saved, I could buy myself a little treat, maybe an ice-cream cone as a reward. I'd earned a treat. I deserved it.

As he neared me, I tensed. It was my money, after all. I worked hard to earn it. I had a right to keep what I'd earned. I had a right to spend it the way I wanted. I shouldn't be expected to give away my hard-earned cash to someone who wasn't working. Braced and tense, I watched as he drew close.

"Can you spare a few cents?" he asked, his hand stretched toward me. I drew back, without actually moving. I thought of the money in my purse. So little of it. And it was mine, all mine.

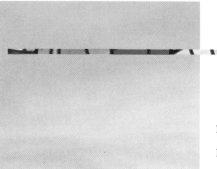

I opened my mouth to make excuses, to tell him I didn't have any money, to lie and brush him away. His eyes pierced mine as I spoke, and I found myself telling him the truth, or at least part of it.

"I don't have much money. Nothing to spare," I told him. In a way, it was true. Money was tight, and I made sacrifices for every treat, like walking those extra blocks to work and back.

Those eyes pierced through my self-satisfaction, my self-righteousness, my selfishness.

"I understand," he told me, his voice deep and steady. And I thought he did understand. Exactly. I thought he saw right through me, into my greedy spirit. I thought he knew somehow just how much money I carried and what I planned to do with it. He seemed to see into my heart and hear the echo of my childish desires. It was my money. I didn't want to share. Why should I? I wanted it for myself.

Then, still holding my gaze, he said, "I have not always been as you see me now," then he walked away, straight backed, dignified in his ragged clothes. He passed behind me, and I stood, stricken and bereft, feeling ashamed of myself.

How could I be so selfish, so greedy, so unkind? Even with so little cash, I could share what I had. I could treat us both to some small treat. We could go together to a nearby snack bar. My money would surely stretch for us both.

In those seconds, I whirled to call him back. He was gone. There was no one behind me. The sidewalk was empty. There were no doorways to slip inside. No cars to duck behind. No alleyways to vanish into. In those moments when I was feeling shame for having been selfish, he'd disappeared.

I never saw him again. But in that moment, staring down an empty sidewalk, I knew. That homeless stranger in his bedraggled clothing had known I wasn't as good and kind and thoughtful as I liked to think I was. He'd known the hidden selfishness in me. He'd known me.

And suddenly I knew him. He'd given me a clue, hadn't he? He'd warned me that he hadn't always been as I saw him then. And I thought of the Bible quote urging hospitality to strangers, that you might be entertaining angels unaware.

For that was what he was. I'm as sure of it as I am of anything. That homeless, ragged stranger, begging coins of me, had been sent to remind me that I was nowhere near as good as I thought I was. He'd pierced my hard and superior attitude.

I thought about those moments for a long time. I rehearsed what I should have told him, what I wished I'd said. I practiced conversations in case he returned to give me another chance. I searched for his face on my walks from then on. But he didn't return. I guess he'd done what he meant to do. He'd taught me a valuable lesson about myself and others. He'd taught me not to think so highly of myself, not to feel so pleased with me. And he taught me not to judge others too easily.

Behind the next stranger in rags there might lurk an angel in disguise.

Sticks and Stones

"Sticks and stones may break my bones,
but words can never hurt me."

Once upon a time, my friend Joan believed that childhood chant. At least, she tried to. When she was young. And plump. And constantly being teased. Then things changed. Joan grew up—and out.

As an adult, she tips the scales at well over 500 pounds. Her friends politely say she's heavy. Her doctor writes "morbidly obese" on her chart. The rest of the world calls her *fat*.

Some people whisper the word. Some people say it out loud, to her face. And, believe it or not, some people say things even worse.

Don't think she hasn't heard the comments. She has. And they hurt. Deeply. But Joan has learned how to avoid the cutting remarks: She simply avoids the people who make them. She stays home.

In her house.

Where it's safe.

But with their 25th wedding anniversary approaching, her husband planned a romantic evening out for the two of them. Knowing it would be difficult, Dan began a persuasive campaign to convince Joan to join him for dinner at a nice restaurant. She agreed.

Reluctantly.

Warily.

To distract herself from fretting about the impending event, Joan, an accomplished seamstress, decided to sew a dressy new blouse for their celebration. All too soon the big night arrived.

At the restaurant, Joan managed to ignore most of the blunt comments. She even managed to disregard the rude stares. But she couldn't overlook the young girl at the table across from them. The youngster never took her eyes off Joan. When the girl headed toward their table, Joan cringed. Experience had taught her that kids could be especially cruel.

The wide-eyed little girl paused next to Joan. Reaching out a single, tentative finger, she touched Joan's indigo velvet blouse.

"You're soft and cuddly, like my bunny," she said.

Joan held her breath while a tiny hand gently stroked her sleeve.

"You're so pretty in that blouse." The little girl smiled and walked back to her seat.

A simple comment. A single compliment.

That was all. But, according to Joan, it was enough to change her life and to alter her perspective.

"Now," Joan says, "when people stare, why, I immediately recall miniature angel fingers caressing my arm. And I'm certain everyone is merely admiring my outfit."

"Now," Joan says, "when people mutter, why, I swear I can hear a young angel's voice reminding me that I'm pretty. And I'm equally sure the words everyone whispers are flattering."

"That's all I hear—now," Joan says, "only compliments. Words that can never hurt me."

Susan's Doll

For ages we have painted angels on ceilings and canvases. For years we have tried to capture their likenesses. We must not forget to put as much effort into understanding and recognizing angels as we have put into how we perceive them.

The day of May 3, 1999, would be scorched on the landscape of my memory for the rest of my life. That was the day that over 70 devastating tornadoes tore across Oklahoma, Kansas, and northern Texas with a ferocity that would claim the lives of more than 45 people. The tornadoes also destroyed thousands of homes and businesses.

As multiple supercell thunderstorms filled the skies just to the east, I hunkered down in my home on the outskirts of the metro Oklahoma City area. Tornado watches became full-fledged warnings. From where I live, I could see the darkening skies miles away, but I breathed with relief when the news alert stated that my area would be safe for now.

Having recently signed up as a Red Cross volunteer, I called the state headquarters and was directed to go to a town ten miles east, to help assess damage and to direct people to the local shelter. When I arrived at the area, I was shocked by what I saw. There were no houses, no trees, no cars parked in driveways. Only devastation and debris piled as high as rooftops. It took me several minutes to get air into my lungs and to stop my legs from shaking after I parked and got out of my car. As I walked along what was once a sidewalk, I saw families huddling, crying, even wailing in agony as they stood before what had once been their homes.

I put on my Red Cross vest and hard hat, and I saw dozens of other volunteers going through the debris. My eyes fell upon a little girl standing with her family. She was maybe five or six, and the pain and terror I saw in her eyes made my heart break.

The little girl's name was Susan, and her family, the Murphys, had lived in their house for more than 20 years. As I led them toward a van that would take them to a local shelter at a nearby elementary school, Susan, crying, broke away and ran back toward the rubble that had once been her home. I motioned for another volunteer to help the rest of the family get in the van as Mrs. Murphy and I ran back to get Susan. Mrs. Murphy spoke softly to her little girl, urging her to come with them and to forget "Ellie." I wondered who Ellie was, perhaps a family pet, and I volunteered to stay behind and look for her. Mrs. Murphy shook her head sadly, telling me Ellie was Susan's doll, and, for all they knew, Ellie had been lifted up into the vortex of the tornado and was now miles away.

As the van drove off, I could not forget the sadness and fear in Susan's innocent eyes. I made a quick check of the house before I headed off to help at the shelter, but I realized it would take several days to find anything amid the heap of walls and floors and furniture, much of which I doubted even belonged to the Murphys.

At the shelter I passed out toiletries and helped set up cots. I spotted the Murphys in a corner, talking quietly. Susan was just staring off into

space. I approached and said hello and asked if there was anything they needed. They thanked me politely for my help and said they were fine. I could see Susan was crying, and I bent down and smiled at her.

"How are you doing, Susan?" I asked. She just nodded, as if to say OK, but I knew she wasn't. I could feel her sadness. "Don't worry, you'll be safe in here," I told her, hoping to alleviate her fears, but she just looked up at me and whispered, "But what about Ellie?" I sat down next to her and asked her what Ellie looked like. Susan's eyes lit up as she described a big cloth doll with brown braids and a freckled nose.

"I'm sure you'll see Ellie again soon," was all I could think of, hoping in my heart that God would work a little magic and make it true. But Susan just looked down and said, "Ellie's gone forever." I didn't know what to say, so I gave her a small hug and moved on. I knew what I had to do. No matter how many people I helped that night, it just wouldn't be enough unless I could make this little girl smile again.

I drove back to where the Murphys' home had once stood. A work camp had been set up, and volunteers and disaster service personnel continued to assess and assist in the cleanup. I knew there was little chance of finding Ellie, but I also knew that if I didn't try, I would never forgive myself.

I put on a pair of thick work gloves and began the slow, tedious effort of looking for a needle in a haystack. I moved aside what debris I could lift, kicked objects over, and peered into dark spaces with my flashlight.

I must have been there for four or five hours. When I finally looked at my watch, it was well past dinnertime but I hadn't felt any hunger. Determined to keep going, I continued my search. I was startled when a male voice behind me boomed, "What are you doing here?" I turned to face a tall, muscular police officer who was glaring at me suspiciously. His badge read "Dan," and I explained that I was looking for something. He asked if I lived here, and I said no, but that I was a friend of the family. That wasn't good enough for him. He informed me that I was trespassing, and he demanded that I leave.

At that moment, I realized that I had a choice. I could just give up and go home to my safe, happy life and forget all about Susan and the doll and all of this terrible damage, or I could do, or at least try to do, something wonderful for someone. I told the officer about Susan, a little girl who was heartbroken without her special doll. To my surprise, Dan offered his help. He got in his patrol car, positioned it toward the rubble, and turned on the high beams. In that light, we searched together for Susan's doll.

I had promised myself that if I didn't find the doll by midnight, I would give up. When midnight passed, I could not let up. Neither could Dan. He used his brute strength to lift doors and broken walls, floorboards and windowpanes. Several times he found toys, but no doll. We could hear his radio in the car announcing calls for assistance. At one point, Dan did have to leave to check on a looting incident a few streets away. He told me he would be back, but I told him not to bother; I would probably be gone by then.

As he drove away, I told myself I would stay one more hour and then it was back to reality. Exhaustion was setting in, and I had only eaten an energy bar all day. Still, I continued to poke and lift and kick over and search. And then I finally called it quits.

There was one thing I had to do before I went home to sleep. I headed back to the shelter and found the Murphys wide awake despite the late hour—refugees who were afraid to close their eyes for fear there might not

be a roof over their heads when they awoke. I sat next to Susan and was about to make up some story about Ellie that I hoped would comfort her when a hand squeezed my shoulder. I looked up to see Dan standing over us. He was holding something in his other hand, and he held it out toward Susan. I was sure her squeals of pleasure would wake folks for miles around. "Ellie!" she shouted over and over again. I stared at Dan and wondered how and where he found it.

He had gone back to the house to find me, and he continued looking. As he lifted up a toppled dresser, he had spotted the doll. Susan held her beloved doll, and her family held each other. I could see the hope in their eyes, and I knew this was the beginning of a journey to healing.

For Susan, that healing would be a bit easier with her faithful companion. I am thankful that a wonderful police officer named Dan refused to give up.

Outward Bound

The phone's ring shattered the silence. Marsha struggled out of the chair to answer it. Her daughter-in-law encouraged Marsha to let the answering machine take the messages, but a lifetime habit was hard to break. She shuffled slowly across the room. Since the stroke her body seemed to continually betray her. She was noticeably out of breath when she answered, "Hello, Biscones."

The cheerful voice on the other end said, "I'd like to speak to Marsha. I'm calling about the information she requested."

Marsha couldn't remember requesting information about anything, but that didn't surprise her. Lots of things seemed to slip by her lately.

"Speaking," she said.

"I'm Liz," said the cheerful voice. "And I'm so glad you're considering Outward Bound. You'll just love the challenge."

Just as Marsha was about to say, "I'm not sure you've got the right person," Liz rushed on. "Lots of folks lack confidence at first. You can push yourself as little or as much as you want to."

Whatever is she talking about, thought Marsha bitterly. If she could just see me, she'd realize I can't do anything!

"Think how proud of your accomplishments you'll feel, Marsha. We all need to be challenged, don't you think?"

Marsha's only thought was that her arm was getting tired holding the phone.

"I can't..." she said.

"Can't is a word we never use," Liz scolded lightly. "Everybody tries their hardest. We aren't all able to climb Mount Everest, but we can all set goals that expand our horizons and increase our stamina."

Marsha sank onto the stool beside the phone. Stamina was not something Marsha had since the stroke.

"Exercise is so energizing," continued Liz.

Exhausting, thought Marsha, or maybe downright dull. Her only exercise consisted of those silly stretches the occupational therapist wanted her to do. I'll just tell this Liz person that I don't want whatever it is she's selling, she thought.

But before she could begin, Liz broke into her thoughts, "And you'll meet such interesting people."

Marsha didn't want to meet anyone. Her son had tried to get her to join a stroke support group when she'd first come to live with them. She'd been adamant. "I'll suffer alone," she'd said. And she had. She supposed her family must be a little tired of hearing her complain. She'd been focusing inward for so long that she hadn't thought much about them.

Liz rattled on. "If you join us, you'll want to bring warm clothes. Banff is beautiful, but it's chilly even in the summer."

Banff? Where had this Liz lady gotten the idea she was going to Banff? She did vaguely remember her grand-

daughter, Marcy, begging her father to let her go to some outdoor camp near there.

"When I send you more information," Liz was still talking, "would you rather I wrote Marsha or Marcy on the envelope?"

Suddenly it was clear. Liz had meant to speak to Marcy. It was to her that Liz had been extolling Outward Bound.

But, thought Marsha, as she explained the misunderstanding, maybe the message had been meant for her. Certainly she'd been focused inward lately.

After she promised to tell Marcy to watch for a packet in the mail, Marsha hung up the phone. Maybe those exercises would be worth doing after all, and maybe she could join that stroke support group. Liz had said everyone needed to be challenged. Marsha would accept the challenge.

I have seen a thousand times that angels are
human forms . . . for I have conversed with them . . .
sometimes with one alone, sometimes with many in company.
Emanuel Swedenborg (1688–1772), Swedish theologian

Angel Baby

If you have the good fortune to be surprised by an angel, you will enjoy a delightful, lingering sense of the divine. Indeed, your life will never be ordinary again.

After a while, you just want to give up and stop trying. At least that's how my husband and I felt after three unsuccessful years of trying to conceive. We had done everything by the book, we were both in excellent shape, still fairly young (in baby-birthing terms, that is!), and tests had turned up nothing unusual. Still, try as we might, we could not get pregnant.

Well-meaning friends and family told us we should adopt, but we really wanted to continue to try for a biological child, at least for now. My husband, John, was as frustrated as I was each time a friend or neighbor in our close-knit Kansas City suburb would offer help. It got harder and harder to listen politely to their advice. No, we did not want a puppy; we wanted a baby! No, fertility drugs were not for us. I was only in my early 30s and healthy as a horse. No, starting a daycare center in my home would not cure my "craving" for a child.

So, three years after we first began our quest for conception, John and I decided to give up. Well, not really. We decided to give it up to God and let nature take whatever course it saw fit. We no longer made love according to a clock or my body temperature, and we no longer bought pregnancy tests every time we went to the market, hoping "this time" it would take. Instead, we focused on living our lives and on leaving the baby game up to a higher power. We knew that God's timing is often different than our own.

24

I had always had what you could describe as clairvoyant dreams. Often, I would dream about a terrible storm or a tornado, and, sure enough, the next day our clear blue Kansas skies would turn dark green. John and I would watch and wait for the severe weather warnings that inevitably drove us into the basement. Luckily, the tornadoes were always far away.

My dreams weren't always of storms. Sometimes I would dream that my mom would call to tell me my father was ill. Sure enough, the next day the phone would ring. I would find out that my pop had another heart attack or pneumonia. In fact, that's how I found out he died. I dreamed he had cardiac failure, and the next day I actually waited for the call to come, fully prepared. I don't really know if it helped or hurt, knowing ahead of time. I knew I should have been grateful that God blessed me with such insight, but the day after my Dad died, I cursed it instead.

But the night I dreamed of the baby with wings, my feelings toward my ability to "dream ahead," as John so succinctly put it, drastically changed. I actually woke up and wondered if it had been a dream at all. It seemed so real to me. I had dreamed of this adorable baby floating above our bed, smiling down at John and me with the most beautiful, glowing face. And it had wings as wispy and transparent as a feather held up to the sun. I thought about waking John that night, but he looked so peaceful. Instead, I decided to wait until the next morning to share my somewhat strange, if not silly, dream with him.

"John, I had another dream last night," I said quietly, "at least, I think it was a dream." He immediately lunged for the window to check the weather. I laughed, assuring him that this time the dream was not about impending natural disaster. I described the baby I had dreamt of, saving the part about the wings for last.

When I was done, John just stared at me for a few moments, his mouth open in a nice little "oh."

"Are you thinking what I'm thinking?" he whispered. And within 15 minutes we were at the market buying another pregnancy test.

Dreams are a funny way for God to communicate with us humans. I was pregnant, all right, at least according to the test. And my own doctor confirmed it three weeks later. John was ecstatic, calling and telling everyone he knew about our good news. That night, as we both lay in bed, I could feel that there was something on his mind. I turned to him and asked what he was thinking about. He looked at me thoughtfully and said, "Any way you could dream up a name for this angel baby?"

Laughing, I grabbed my pillow and smacked him playfully, knowing that if I gave my dreams time, they would answer all of my questions, maybe even all of my prayers.

One Less Load

I hadn't even noticed my clothes until then. They definitely had the "slept-in look." But then, they had been slept in! Ever since we'd brought our baby, Lisa, to Children's Hospital, either Frank or I had been by her bedside. The hospital had encouraged us to take advantage of the Ronald McDonald house, but that seemed too far away from her hospital bed. It was even hard for me to leave Lisa alone long enough to go to the bathroom. Only now with her condition stabilized did I allow myself to think of the world outside the hospital and of my home and family.

How lucky we'd been to have thoughtful friends and neighbors. They'd brought in meals and cared for our four other children. And there had been lots of other people who'd promised help if we needed it.

Looking at my skirt, I was reminded that I hadn't done the wash for days. The kids had surely run out of clothes. Whatever must the teachers be thinking of our two school-age children. Though Mike, eight years old, was probably delighted that he hadn't had to change for two weeks, by now he must be starting to smell!

I could go home for a few hours, I thought, and do the wash. The doctors had assured us that Lisa was out of danger. She would probably not wake until morning, and Frank was asleep in the waiting room. I knew the nurses would wake him if she did begin to fuss.

I walked through the frigid January darkness to our car. My breath fogged the windows. I turned on the defroster to clear them. My mind cleared, too. For the first time, I could look back on the last weeks and think about all that had happened.

As I drove the two hours to our home outside Denver, I recalled rushing our ashen baby to Children's Hospital after our local doctor diagnosed heart failure. The heart specialist said that without surgery Lisa would die. And surgery was risky. She was so tiny, only 13 pounds at 6 months, and her condition was so unstable. The medical team opted to wait a few days, hoping to strengthen her before putting her under anesthesia.

We signed the papers okaying the surgery scheduled three days later, but both of us tried to ignore the survival statistics. We waited. The doctors wanted Lisa kept quiet because movement and activity made her heart work harder. Crawling at home, they said, was what had put her heart into overload. It had been exhausting keeping her entertained while curtailing her movement. We tried to get her to eat more and drink less because sucking her bottle took too much energy. She'd cry in frustration and exhaustion after only an ounce or two. Ice cream was our salvation. We spoon-fed her frozen formula every two to three hours while we waited for the surgery.

As I turned off the highway, my reverie continued. I allowed myself to think back to the most frightening day of all. It was the day before the doctors planned to operate. I was rocking Lisa while the late afternoon sunshine streamed into the room. Suddenly I realized something was dreadfully wrong. Her little lips were turning blue. Frantic, I paged the nurse. She gasped when she saw Lisa. Doctors and nurses rushed in. The surgery could not be postponed. They wheeled her away.

Frank and I sat alone in fear as we waited out the six-hour surgery. We stood up, side by side, when we saw the green-clad surgeon striding into the ICU waiting room. He did not smile reassuringly. They had been able to close the hole in Lisa's heart, but she still might not pull through. The next few hours would tell. They'd keep her in the recovery room so they could constantly monitor her vital signs. We watched the clock and waited. After what seemed an eternity, a volunteer came to tell us they had moved Lisa upstairs.

How we rejoiced! And now in a few days we would be traveling this very road to bring our baby back home. Then perhaps our lives could return to normal. Then maybe I wouldn't be driving home in the middle of the night to do the wash.

I parked in front of the garage. I'd given up control so completely that I had no idea who was there with the kids, but I didn't want them to be startled by the sound of the garage door opening. Whatever had possessed me to come, I wondered, as I tiptoed into the dark house. I switched on the light in the dining room. A pile of mail lay on the table, awaiting a neighbor who worked in Denver. He dropped it off at the hospital each day. Beside the mail I saw an amazing sight: stacks of clean, folded clothes.

On the top of one pile was this poem signed by a kindly older neighbor.

> I used to say to folks like you,
> "Please let me know what I can do.
> I'd like to help, I really would,
> If you'd just tell me how I could."
> But then I began to see that
> chances to serve God were passing me.
> So now I try to do small things,
> perhaps they'll help me earn my wings.

I put away the folded clothes but not the poem. Instead I posted it on my kitchen bulletin board. Before Lisa's surgery I'd been a person who said, "Just let me know how I can help." From now on I would not wait to be told.

We can learn much more from angels about goodness and light than we will ever learn from this incandescent world in which we exist.

Supermarket Angel

As a young mother of two growing boys, Gina often had to struggle to make ends meet, especially on her weekly grocery trip. She and her husband, Jim, a police officer, had worked out a budget that, if they stuck to diligently, would allow them to someday buy a home of their own.

So it surprised her that on this particular shopping trip she would feel compelled to do what she was about to do. As her boys fought over who would unload the cart, Gina noticed the person ahead of her in the checkout line.

By his ragged clothes and dirty, disheveled appearance, she could see that the man was homeless. His hair was knotted and greasy, and he obviously had not bathed in a while. Normally, Gina would just ignore homeless people, not because she was rude, but because she, like so many other people, didn't know how to react. And perhaps there was that fear deep down inside her that if Jim ever lost his job, she, too, could be homeless.

Still, today something forced her to pay attention. When she saw his meager basket filled with nothing but a loaf of bread, a can of tuna, two apples, and a bottle of water, her heart broke wondering how long this food would have to last him. When she heard the checker lean toward the old man and whisper to him that he did not have enough money to pay for the food—and she saw the fallen look in the old man's eyes—Gina decided to do something she had never done before.

Angels give their best to help us do our best.

Despite the nasty grumbling of the people standing behind Gina, who were annoyed at the holdup, and despite going over her budget, Gina asked the checker to wait. She took out her wallet and quietly offered to pay for the man's food. She held her breath and hoped he would accept her offer. She could feel her boys become very quiet, watching as the checker slowly took the money.

The checker looked stunned, as if no one had ever done this before, but the old man looked at Gina with eyes brimming with tears of gratitude. Gina looked into his eyes, really seeing the human being behind them. When he whispered his words of thanks, she smiled and replied, "It's my pleasure." The old man continued to thank her profusely, even offering her the couple of dollars he did have, but Gina refused, hoping her small gesture would offer him more than food for a few days. She hoped it would offer him hope. She didn't need his few dollars—her heart and her basket were already overflowing.

As she pushed the cart to her car and saw the proud looks on the faces of her two young boys, Gina knew that her simple gesture of kindness had not been lost on them. She realized that there was nothing more powerful than the act of giving, no matter how small or insignificant the gift might seem. She drove home filled with the joy of knowing that, even if only for a day, she could be someone else's angel.

Angels in Action

Have you ever met a hero? I have. I have seen him, touched him, fought with him, laughed at him, cried with him, and even given birth to his children. Of course, I married him first— five years before I even knew he was a hero.

On the night I realized he was a hero, I held my breath in anticipation as he walked back to me, backlit by a spectrum of emergency vehicle flashing lights. He was covered in blood and looked like any good action hero in the last frames of some nerve-tweaking adventure film. And now I know what happens to the hero in the minutes, hours, days, months, and years to follow. Do you know what he does, that dashing man with all the finesse and wisdom? He drives his used car back to his parents' house with his pregnant wife and becomes a normal man once again.

This all happened when we were coming home from my cousin's wedding. I was five months pregnant and had stayed out too late for my growing body. I had changed into sweat clothes for the hour-long drive back to my in-laws' house, where we planned to spend the rest of the weekend relaxing. My husband—a mild-mannered, soft-spoken man named Jon— was quietly driving along a stretch of dark road, still wearing his tuxedo. There was little traffic on this two-lane roadway; we were about five miles outside the nearest small town. Empty farm fields surrounded us. Cranky and tired, I tried to settle in for a nap. I started to close my eyes when I saw a flicker of bright lights up ahead.

As we neared the lights, I saw the man we would later know as Mr. Smith. When I first saw him, he looked ghoulish. His white face and hollow eyes made him appear as if he were wearing a Halloween mask. As we pulled up alongside him, Jon rolled down the window, and I heard words I still hear in nightmares almost ten years later: "Please help me. We've been hit, and my wife is trapped under the van. I just found my daughter."

The man waved wildly toward what we could see were the remains of a once-stylish recreational vehicle. Now it looked like the loser in a demolition derby. Panicked by these sudden frightening events, I could neither speak nor move. Tears openly poured down Mr. Smith's face as he stood there, waiting for us to respond. Soon a horn began to honk behind us.

"I'm a nurse," my husband said calmly but firmly. He got out of the car and, reaching back in, kissed me with a quick fierceness I had rarely felt. I began to cry. As he walked away, he instructed me to get help, then left me in the car, enveloped by complete darkness. By the time I drove to the nearest farmhouse, I was swallowing huge, hitching sobs.

The house was guarded by a number of large farm dogs who quickly surrounded my car. I honked the horn repeatedly as my tires rolled in the gravel driveway. By the time I reached the house, a large man was standing right behind the screen door. As I

approached him, babbling hysterically, the man appeared far too calm to be really listening. "Hush!" he yelled, and the dogs and I all quieted instantly. The man told me he was a dispatcher for the local emergency services, and, as he said it, I could hear the crackle and buzz of a police scanner buried in the house somewhere.

"You go on back now. I'll call in and follow," he said, closing the door in my face. I had to take him at his word. I raced back to the car, still sobbing, and tripped over one of the dogs, who nipped at my ankle. Unthinking and almost blind with fear, I swung my handbag at the mongrel, and he yelped as he limped out of my way. It was the first time I had ever hurt an animal on purpose. This night was filled with many "firsts" for me.

I was a geriatric social worker; I took care of people's emotions and fought wars on paper. I had dealt with many emergencies, but I always had easy access to resources—to professionals like my husband. He was a nurse in the intensive care unit at a large trauma center. He had just completed his master's degree in nursing and was halfway through his internship in anesthesia. Every week seemed to contain at least two or three radical medical emergencies that he had to deal with. Until now, for me, those emergencies had been stories told over dinner in a safe, warm home far from the hospital. But this was not a story, and Mr. Smith was not a nameless, faceless patient. I drove faster.

A bottleneck of cars had formed at the spot where the overturned van leaned in and out of the ditch at the same time. I yelled, "Help is on the way!" into the darkened night. "I'm an EMT," I heard a man shout as he hastily parked and ran out to help. I could not see my husband. I turned my headlights to the particular patch of darkness I believed to be the epicenter of activity. "Thank you very much. It's about time," I heard Jon yell to the approaching medical technician. "Hey! The girl needs help. Hey! Mom!" he shouted. "There's another man here who can help. Wave or something so he knows where he needs to go." As an afterthought, and in what I knew to be his generous manner, Jon added, "We're doing fine over here, Mr. Smith. You're doing a great job taking care of your daughter." But I knew from the false tone of cheer in his voice that things were not going all that well. He was afraid, but he was trying not to show it. The sanitized, plastic-wrapped instruments he was accustomed to using were unavailable. His hands, experience, and education, combined with the contents of the cars belonging to the few persons who stopped to help, were all the resources he had until more help arrived.

I tried to walk to the front of the damaged van. But the very sight of blood made me nauseous, and I knew I would be more of a liability than a help at that point. More people stopped, but still no emergency vehicles came to our rescue.

I began to walk along the shoulder of the road, picking up littered pieces of these people's lives. A small shoe, a lawn chair, a box of papers, a blanket. These were items that belonged to real people. With each item I piled up, I said a prayer. God and I talked a lot that night.

And then, finally, the police came, and the story slowly unfolded. A man who had been drinking heavily plowed into the side of the Smiths' van and then drove away. He did not have a current license since he'd had a previous DUI. He was found two hours later at another bar, still drink-

Angels follow our steps as clearly as if we were forever walking in newly fallen snow.

ing and totally unaware that the accident had happened. But he'd been traced by the license plate and vehicle parts left behind at the crash site. He had never even missed them.

The ambulance arrived, and, through the confusion, I heard my husband's authoritative voice barking orders for tubes and lines and bags. He was running the show, without a twinge of doubt about malpractice or lack of training. There was no one else to take charge, so he stepped up without giving it a second thought.

Mrs. Smith was trapped under the wheels of the van. She had no airway, an erratic pulse, and was unconscious. We were waiting for the tow truck to lift the vehicle off her upper body. The ambulance crew doubted she'd make it to the trauma center. My husband assured them that she would. He did in that field what he would have done in the ICU or in the OR: He kept her alive. And with all this on his shoulders, I could hear Jon reassuring Mr. Smith that his wife could still hear him so he should talk to her calmly and hold her hand. I can only imagine how precious those moments were for Mr. and Mrs. Smith. As promised, she was stabilized and placed in the ambulance for an hour-long drive to the waiting hospital. Their daughter rode in another ambulance, not faring much better.

And that's when I saw my husband as more than just a man who forgets to hang up towels and tracks mud on the carpet. I saw a hero. And I thanked God for him. Later, as I cleaned the blood out of his tuxedo shirt in the basement of his parents' home, I cried and prayed. Again.

Mrs. Smith was stabilized on the way to the trauma center, as my husband had promised she would be, and rushed into the operating room. She died the next morning. It was a hollow victory at best. Her 12-year-old daughter survived and, after many months of medical care and rehabilitation, was able to resume a somewhat normal life.

When I read Mrs. Smith's obituary, I cried as if I had lost a friend. I wrote a note to Mr. Smith, telling him how sorry we were and assuring him that his wife had known he was there in those final moments. I sent it to the funeral home and did not expect a response.

Two weeks later I received a letter with an unfamiliar return address. It was from Mr. Smith. He wrote a long outpouring of love and loss and thankfulness concerning his beloved wife. He explained that she had been a full-time schoolteacher and part-time college professor, and he talked about her kindness and "humanness."

He thanked us for helping and called us...angels.

And for some people, that ends the story. Some step back, take a look at the destruction, and say, "See, God lets bad things happen to good people." And I absolutely agree. God never promises in the Bible that bad things will never happen to you because you are his. He only promises that he will be there by your side every step of the way if they do.

Mr. Smith and his daughter are survivors. Mr. Smith became a fighter in the cause against drunk driving. I am sure there is at least one student, one secretary, one judge, or one jury member who has stopped driving dangerously since hearing Mr. Smith's testimonies. Many classes of children lost a woman they loved to a drunk driver. I am sure they now think before drinking.

That night changed the lives of so many people, including my husband's and mine. Things certainly aren't perfect for us, and we have our own struggles. But even in the toughest times, I can still see my husband as the hero. He is an angel in the truest sense of the word.

Angels move in mysterious and wonderful ways. They speak with hushed and holy voices, and in warm and gentle tones. Their loving presence and kind words cover us with peace and comfort.

From the Heart of a Child

The storms that hit the counties east of us were the most devastating we had ever known in the state of Oklahoma. While our own neighborhoods were spared, we had to watch as towns just miles away were flattened. I tried to spare my eight-year-old daughter, Amy, from the horror, but she heard about it from her schoolmates and insisted on watching the local evening news.

Amy watched, transfixed, as the reporters showed the extensive damage and the stunned, frightened families that no longer had homes to call their own. One newswoman focused on the family of a young boy named Rodney. The boy was devastated at the loss of his new puppy, Albert. The little beagle had panicked and escaped from the cellar where the family was hiding when a twister smashed through their house. Albert was lifted by the strong winds and thrown into a wall, his body limp and lifeless when rescue workers found him.

Amy sat silently for the longest time after seeing that report. She seemed lost in thought, so I didn't question her when she ran into her room and closed the door. My husband volunteered to console her, but when he opened her bedroom door, she wasn't crying. She was counting money on her bedspread. Her broken ceramic angel bank lay beside her, and, as we came in, Amy looked up at us with huge, hopeful eyes and told us her plan.

She intended to use her $4.12 to buy a new puppy for Rodney. I immediately tried to talk her out of it, informing her that the boy had no home to keep the dog in, and that the price of a new beagle was way more than what she could afford. Purebred pups went for several hundred dollars. But Amy wouldn't hear of my adult excuses. She just shook her head and said that there were plenty of nice puppies at the local pound and that surely there would be a beagle there.

My husband looked at me with one of those what-do-we-do-now looks, and I shrugged, hoping that as the days passed Amy would forget all about Rodney and Albert and beagle puppies. But three days later, Amy was tugging at my blouse, asking if today was the day we would go and pick out the puppy. I barely got out a protest when the phone rang. I answered it, surprised to find myself talking to the news reporter who had told Rodney's story on TV!

Apparently, Amy had called the news station herself and asked for the reporter, who had been out on a story at the time. Now, the woman, Linda Hayes, was telling me all about Rodney's family and what shelter they were staying at and how wonderful she thought my daughter was to use her own money to make a little boy happy.

What could I say, except that, yes, my daughter really was pretty wonderful. I arranged a time to meet Linda and her camera crew at the local

animal shelter. When we arrived, Amy raced off to look for the perfect gift. I shouted after her, but she was nowhere to be found until Linda's camera operator spotted her playing with a tiny puppy in a cage.

"Mama, look! He's perfect!" Amy shouted, pleading with her eyes for me to hurry and come see the adorable beagle pup that licked Amy's hand lovingly. At that moment, a shelter worker came up to us and asked if we wanted to meet Rudy. Amy squealed with delight as the woman let Rudy out to meet us. The puppy ran immediately to Amy and begged to be picked up. As Amy held the puppy, rocking it back and forth, I had a funny feeling that I would be buying not one, but two puppies that day.

As we paid for Rudy, Linda did a news report and interviewed Amy. I had whispered to Linda that I wanted to surprise my daughter with a pup of her own and that it might be fun to reveal our secret on camera. But Amy never gave her a chance. She was intent on delivering Rudy to Rodney. Linda looked at me, and I nodded that we would go to Plan B.

Later that day, we went to Red Rock Elementary School, the temporary shelter where Rodney's family was staying. Linda found the family, and we quietly talked with the parents about Amy's intentions, hoping they would be open to the idea despite the tremendous loss they had suffered. Not only were they open to it, they were grateful to the point of tears, amazed that a little girl had cared enough to do something special for their child.

Rodney sat quietly nearby, but the minute Amy walked up to him with Rudy in her arms the light went on in his gray-blue eyes. He stared at the dog, as if in shock. Amy handed the pup over and whispered, "He's yours.

His name is Rudy, but you can call him Albert if you want to." There was not a dry eye in the shelter as Rodney and Rudy were introduced and an instant bond of love and friendship was formed.

It was a scene my family would watch again later that evening on the local news. Watching Amy smile at Rodney playing with his new puppy made my heart swell. I could barely keep from bursting into tears.

My husband went outside, and he yelled for Amy to come out into the backyard. When I got up to follow and saw the look on Amy's face as she was presented with a yapping little beagle pup, my tears let loose like a waterfall. I was so filled with joy and pride and gratitude as I watched a very special little girl fall in love with a puppy of her own.

Faithful Angels

Twists and turns, corners we

cannot negotiate. This is the nature

of an angel's world: Helping us

with the unknown challenges as

well as the ones that stare

us in the face.

SUV Angel

*S*am Edwards looked longingly at the big, new sport utility vehicle, a shiny rolling fortress that can go just about anywhere. A lawyer, he pictured leaving behind his three-piece suits and piles of contracts for wild places. Strike off into the forest! Conquer mountains! That's what he imagined as he announced to the salesperson that he would take it.

Sam proudly drove the 4×4 home. "Cool!" his teenage son exclaimed. His wife just smiled and shook her head. Everyone at the firm praised his choice. But as time passed, Sam never seemed to have time to do the fun things he had dreamed about. He reluctantly admitted to himself that the 4×4 might have been an expensive mistake.

Then, the snow began one January night and kept falling until the next morning. When Sam rose at 5:30 A.M., he found the world swathed in white. "Must be more than a foot!" he thought gleefully, eager to test his SUV against the elements. Just as he was ready to head out the door, the phone rang. It was his firm's managing partner with news the office would shut down for the day. Sam said he might go in anyway. "Well, they're saying to stay off the roads, but it's up to you," his boss replied.

Sam poured a cup of coffee and stared out the window. It's silly to be disappointed, he admonished himself.

Half an hour later, the phone rang again. It was Linda, his neighbor. He started to say that his wife wasn't up yet, but she interrupted.

"It's you I need to speak to. Do you still have that big truck thing—the one with 4-wheel drive?" she inquired briskly.

"Sure," Sam answered, wondering where this conversation was headed.

"Can I catch a ride to work?" she asked. "They really need me—hardly anyone is making it in, and there have been accidents all over town."

"Uh...I...uh...where?" Sam hesitated, about to explain that he was not going in to work himself. He was also embarrassed that he didn't know what Linda did.

"The emergency room at County. They really need me to come in."

"Sure," Sam replied, "give me ten minutes."

Pulling out of the garage into the drifts that obscured his driveway, Sam realized that he had never used the SUV's 4-wheel-drive capability. He worried whether he could maneuver in a foot of snow with no experience. "Slow and steady," he decided, rumbling down the block.

Bundled head to foot, Linda waded through knee-deep snow and climbed in, brushing the snow from her jacket. "Do you mind making a couple of stops?" she asked hopefully. "One of the doctors and another nurse."

"Well, sure," Sam was even more willing to help now that he was out of the house and embarking on this mini-adventure. "Just point me in the right direction."

The streets were in the worst shape he'd ever seen. Drivers had given up battling the drifts and had abandoned their cars, leaving them to form

a snow-covered obstacle course that blocked traffic lanes wherever Sam turned. Picking up the others and driving across town—a 20-minute trip—took an hour and a half. Sam was relieved to see the flashing "Emergency" sign through the sleet. He drew a deep breath and stretched his aching muscles, which had cramped up because he had been sitting in one position for so long. His passengers climbed out, thanking him again and again.

Sam felt good, but he was anxious to get home. He'd had quite enough 4-wheeling in the elements for one day. But just as he was about to pull away, Linda ran up and knocked on the window.

Her look said it all. "The people we're replacing are exhausted, but some of them don't have a way to get home. Do you think you could...?"

"Sure thing," Sam said again, putting aside a mental image of a good book and his chair in front of the fire.

All day, Sam ferried doctors, nurses, and other workers back and forth to the hospital. Several other SUVs seemed to be doing the same thing.

He took Linda home on his final run. The snow had been falling all day, and the street crews hadn't made much of a dent in the mess.

"Tomorrow...is there any way...?" Linda asked hesitantly.

"Is 6:00 A.M. all right?" Sam asked immediately.

A few days after the crisis, Sam called Linda with a suggestion. She jumped on the idea and took it to her superiors. The neighbors worked to organize volunteer SUV drivers. Thanks to Sam and Linda, a corps of SUVs now stands ready, with drivers on 24-hour call, to help transport vital medical personnel to the hospital during weather emergencies.

Sometimes angels need to provide transportation.

The angel on your shoulder whispers in your ear: "You are loved, so love others. You are blessed, so bless others. You are my friend, so be a friend."

Good Girl, Hattie

Ralph volunteered to string the Christmas lights on the trees in the common ground of his subdivision.

He brushed aside his neighbors' thanks. A building contractor, it was no big deal for him to climb up on a ladder, even during the coldest November on record. In fact, he rather enjoyed the time to himself, reflecting on the joys of the season and the blessings that filled his life. He brought his dog, Hattie, along with him for some company.

Ralph had lots of experience working high off the ground—perhaps too much, he later reflected. Maybe he had become overconfident.

He was standing on one of the highest rungs, reaching to hook a strand around a branch at the back of a tall tree, when he lost his balance. He fell to the frozen ground with a sickening crunch, landing with his leg folded behind him. Searing pain gripped him when he tried to move.

"That leg's broken," Ralph moaned. The only question was whether he could make his way home. Gingerly trying to pull the leg out from under him, he grimaced in pain. There was no way he could even move, let alone make it all the way back to the road where someone could see him.

"Someone will come along," he told himself, trying to think positively despite the gathering dusk and deepening cold. He rubbed his hands together, trying in vain to keep warm. Hattie nuzzled his face and barked uneasily.

"Very tired . . . I'll just rest," Ralph mumbled to himself. Almost as soon as he dozed off, a persistent sound brought him back. "That darn

dog...always barking...." Barking and whining, Hattie demanded that Ralph get up and come home before he froze to death.

"Home, Hattie," Ralph's words sounded slurred, even to himself. Ralph hoped his weak command would send Hattie on her way, and maybe his family would realize he was missing when they saw the dog. "Go home."

Looking cowed, Hattie finally trotted off.

"Probably headed straight for her favorite spot by the fire," Ralph thought, shivering uncontrollably.

But Hattie ran straight to Ralph's backyard and started barking. She wouldn't stop, even when they let her in, put out her supper dish, and petted her. She kept up the shrill, incessant barking, running back and forth in front of the door.

Mary, Ralph's wife, came to the kitchen to see what the commotion was about. Hattie barked even louder and pawed the door.

"You crazy dog," Mary exclaimed, exasperated. "Is there something out there that you want? What is it—a squirrel?"

Hattie stood her ground and whined, then barked some more.

Looking at the clock, Mary suddenly realized that Ralph wasn't home yet. "Where's Ralph?" she asked uneasily. This time,

when Hattie barked louder, Mary opened the kitchen door and followed as Hattie charged out and raced across the lawn. Mary sped after her, trying to keep up.

By the time Mary reached Ralph, he was half frozen. Even a strong man can stand only so much cold and pain. At the hospital, his recovery was slow, with doctors watching closely to see if he would regain full use of his frozen fingers.

Today, Hattie still barks at the mail carrier, birds and squirrels, and nothing in particular. "You bark all you want to, big girl," Ralph says, patting his angel, and Mary agrees wholeheartedly.

Angels are the ministers and the dispensers of the divine bounty toward us. Accordingly, we are told how they watch for our own safety, how they undertake our defense, direct our path, and take heed that no evil befall us.

John Calvin, Institute of the Christian Religion, Vol. 1

A Big Man

*I*ce—huge chunks that could punch holes in a boat's bow or shove it wrecked against the shore—threatened traffic on the Mississippi River that frigid night. Cargoes, boats, and whole crews had been known to become lost in conditions like these. But river men tried not to think about the worst. Lights scanned the black waters ahead, and pilots strained to see. Ice warnings were radioed to all boats within hearing distance.

In better weather, old boats, permanently moored and set up as supply stations at ports along the river, broadcast information on conditions. But tonight the ice threatened even those vessels, and most operators shut down and went ashore. Captains held their breaths approaching the Mississippi's treacherous junction with the Ohio River. If only they knew what to expect!

Just when each captain had resigned to navigating the passage blind, a deep, reassuring baritone crackled over the radio: "Downbound . . . any downbound boats. This is Cairo supply station." It was the operator that river men had nicknamed "Big Voice," renowned for his powerful voice and his meticulous reports on river conditions. He was still on the air!

Captains almost leaped for joy, not quite able to believe that Big Voice hadn't abandoned his old boat and headed for safety.

With calm authority, Big Voice described a narrow passage through the massing ice, relaying reports from boats that had already made the run.

The night wore on, and Big Voice kept broadcasting, a lifeline for the half-dozen boats and their crews that were attempting to navigate the treacherous junction. When he suddenly lost touch with one boat, Big Voice radioed for rescue crews and then announced triumphantly over the air that the crew had been plucked from the freezing water.

As dawn broke gray and dim, signaling an end to the river men's ordeal, the voice went silent. Grateful captains assumed Big Voice had signed off for some much-deserved rest.

A few hours later, the captain of the boat that had wrecked went in search of Big Voice, intending to thank him for his help. The captain discovered the old boat shoved onto shore, with a jagged tear in its bow; it was tilting precariously toward the raging, icy river. Before long, the old junker would plunge into the river and sink. The captain hesitated to board the near-foundering craft—surely anyone on board would have disembarked by now. But something told him he should take a look around.

"Hello!" he called into the dark interior. "Anyone on board?"

"Over here. I'm over here!" The captain recognized the calm, powerful voice.

Puzzled, he threaded his way through the dim, musty interior.

"Over here, behind the desk," the voice said. "Lucky you showed up. I sure could use some help."

The captain peered over the desk, and tears sprang to his eyes at what he saw. A wheelchair lay overturned, and a frail young man, not more than 20 years old, had pulled himself up on one arm and was struggling into a sitting position, dragging withered legs.

Bright beings, dazzling as lightning; glorious angels, shimmering like the sun; powerful spirits, descending from heaven; swift presence, visible and invisible.

"You're Big Voice!" the captain exclaimed.

"I guess that's what they call me," the young man answered, looking embarrassed. "I guess some ice hit the boat, and I was knocked out of my chair. I'm sorry I couldn't stay on the air longer."

"You're helpless on a sinking boat, and you're worried about us out there," the captain said, shaking his head in wonder. He righted the chair and lifted the shivering young man, wrapping a blanket around him. "I've been on the river most of my life—in plenty of bad spots, worse even than last night—but you make me feel small, son. You make me feel small."

Cheers for the Bus Driver

Dorothy perches on the edge of the porch bench, feet gently tapping on the terra cotta bricks of the patio as she waits patiently for her ride. It's Tuesday, and there should be a new delivery of peaches at her favorite farmstand. Thank goodness! With the church bake sale coming up in just a couple days, Dorothy had started to worry that she wouldn't be able to bake her renowned peach pie as she had done for more years than she cared to remember.

She sighs. Until she failed her driving test last year—at the age of 85!—she hadn't realized how dependent she was on her car. She used it to run errands, visit friends, and—especially—to drive across town to the movie theater. Dorothy tried to remember the last time she'd been to a movie. She used to see almost every new release, but now it's been a while since she's seen any movie at all. When she lost her license, she lost more than the ability to drive. She also lost her independence—her freedom. She still has the energy and the desire to bake pies, go to the movies, and socialize with her friends, but she no longer has the means to do these things.

She sighs again, then begins to smile as she sees a familiar van pull around the corner and turn into her driveway. Anne waves and grins from behind the wheel. "Come on," she calls. "The movie starts in an hour, and Sean Connery's not going to wait around for you forever!"

Dorothy gathers her purse, straightens her hat, and starts down the steps, grinning.

When Dorothy first met Anne through her church, she took an immediate liking to the energetic, friendly young woman. As their friendship developed, Dorothy began to recognize that Anne, who had never known her own grandparents, delighted in "adopting" surrogate grandparents. That was just fine with Dorothy, who already felt a strong tie to Anne.

When Anne saw Dorothy's despondence over losing her license, Anne got an idea. In no time, it seemed, she went to school and obtained a license permitting her to drive vans and even buses. Anne now uses this license to give joy to senior citizens, Dorothy included. Anne cheerfully chauffeurs her friends around on errands, but she also racks her brain to plan fun, worthwhile activities for them to enjoy. Some of their favorite excursions have been to the local zoo, a doll museum, the beach, and the glorious flower fields at the Botanic Gardens.

As Dorothy carefully steps into the van, ready for their outing—first to see the latest summer blockbuster and then on to the farmstand to take care of business—she reflects that Anne has been much more than a chauffeur for her. She is also her friend—her angel.

The Flower Lady

Flowering plants didn't show up on the earth until relatively late in the planet's life.

Evolutionist Charles Darwin is said to have called flowers "an abominable mystery," because "they appeared so suddenly and spread so fast."

Lifelong gardener Margie McLean would say that flowers' real mystery is their ability to lift the human spirit.

She learned to grow towering irises and lush beds of roses as a child watching her grandmother tend the garden that grew next to their Midwest farmhouse.

When Margie moved to Atlanta, she planted a large garden and grew more flowers than she could have imagined back home. She planted more beds each year, and the yard became a kaleidoscope of color. Sweet fragrances perfumed the air.

Margie gave flowers to her neighbors, but that did not satisfy her urge to spread the joy the flowers brought her. One day, she hit on the notion of delivering blooms to a nearby nursing home. She arranged the flowers in bouquets just as a florist would. Nurses pointed her toward lonely residents who would appreciate the flowers. Margie stopped for a few minutes to visit as she made each delivery. Some understood that the flowers were from her; others imagined that they had come from loved ones. It didn't matter; the looks of pure joy on the seniors' faces were thanks enough.

The deliveries became a weekly ritual. Margie enclosed cards that addressed residents by name and included encouraging personal messages.

"Hope you're feeling better this week, Bert! Love, Margie" one card said.

"Thanks for your wonderful smile!" another card praised a gentleman who always seemed cheerful despite his infirmities.

Nurses now alert the "Flower Lady," as residents call her, to bring special bouquets when a resident needs a lift.

Margie says, "There's nothing like a bouquet of flowers to show someone that he or she is loved."

Celestial beings, messengers of light, the neighbor next door, even a passing stranger—angels come to us in many forms. Be open to receive them.

Street Angel

*I*nsomnia is a lonely, restless affliction. Chronically unable to sleep, Joe Masters walked the streets of the big city that was his hometown. Eventually, his wanderings took him farther and farther into neighborhoods where he had not ventured before.

He would start out in the dark and walk for two, maybe three hours. At first, he was barely aware of his surroundings or the people he passed. One night, however, he realized with a start that the same people were leaning in the same doorways and bus shelters night after night. He looked more closely at their layers of worn clothing. They were homeless, of course, a condition that Joe, a successful insurance salesman, had only read about. Joe began to nod and say hello as he recognized familiar faces. Sometimes his greetings were returned.

One blustery March night, Joe came across a man he had seen several times before, slumped on the steps of an old building. Other nights, the man had seemed friendly. Tonight, he barely nodded when Joe said hi. In a flash, Joe realized the man might be weak from hunger. He dug through his parka pockets and found a candy bar. He offered it reluctantly, embarrassed that it looked as if it had been in his pocket for awhile. The man took it gratefully, thanking Joe so sincerely that Joe felt even worse that he didn't have more to offer.

From then on, Joe filled his pockets with candy and fruit and began directing his walks to the neighborhoods where he knew he would

An angel of compassion is like a bowl of chicken soup made by Mom. It makes you feel all warm inside. It makes you feel loved.

encounter homeless, hungry people. Soon he was toting a backpack filled with sandwiches and other easy-to-carry foods. He developed a regular route. His new friends waited anxiously for his visits.

Joe had become a walking food pantry. Somehow, the word got out. Other people offered to help. A grocer provided day-old bread and sandwich meat. Donations of more food and money trickled in.

Sometimes Joe didn't feel up to the journey, but he went anyway, not wanting to let down his street friends. Before he knew it, Joe was feeding 100 people a night.

Not every night has been smooth. He has faced threats and, once, a knife-wielding mugger. A big man, Joe says, "I can take care of myself, but it's usually not necessary. I know that these people are suffering, and they act out of fear." The people he feeds say thank you, but Joe brushes gratitude aside. "I feel fortunate I can help," he says.

Sometimes people want to talk even more than they want something to eat. Life on the streets is lonely. Joe offers a hug or a handshake to anyone who seems to need one.

Drugs and alcohol often add to the street people's suffering. Joe listens patiently, and he carries a list of agencies that can help if the person is willing.

Once in a while he sees that his efforts have made a difference. One night a man pulled up in a newer-model car, announcing that he'd been looking for Joe all over. "Don't you recognize me?" he asked with mock indignation, handing Joe a check. "That's the money you lent me and more. Without it I couldn't have turned things around."

Friends marvel at Joe's seven-day-a-week schedule. People ask what keeps him going. Joe turns his eyes upward and says simply, "I sincerely believe that he walks with me." Some nights, Joe admits, he's so weary he can barely finish his route. "You know," he says with an easy smile, "I never have trouble sleeping anymore."

Who are these godly beings that minister to us? They are wise and wonderful personalities that come before us in visions, in dreams, and in person.

Feeding Angels

It will not bother me in the hour of death to reflect that I have been "had for a sucker" by any number of impostors; but it would be a torment to know that one had refused even one person in need.
C.S. Lewis, *Letters to an American Lady*

I fed an angel today! At least I may have.

"I won't hurt you, lady." The kind face behind the voice seemed incapable of harm. My heart beat wildly as the story unfolded. He hadn't eaten in two days. His hunger was evident. Vacant, hollow eyes waited for my response. I knew what Jesus would do, but was I brave enough to follow through?

My mind and brain functioned in tandem. "I'll buy you lunch," I said, "but I can't give you any money." Why did I say that? It seemed to be the right thing to say.

I wondered if I was "being taken." Like a grateful puppy, the man waited for me to buy the food, and he accepted it with murmured thanks. I awkwardly grasped for conversation.

When we parted, I knew I had done the right thing. Onlookers at the restaurant nodded approval. A restaurant worker tipped his hat to me. One human being helping another…is that *so* unusual that the world notices?

I never saw the man again. Professional huckster or tramp? Was I "Ms. Gullible"? Perhaps.

I guess I'll never know for sure. But today I fed an angel, and I prefer to think of it that way.

Do not neglect to show hospitality to strangers, for by doing that some have entertained angels without knowing it.

Hebrews 13:2

Messenger Angels

Life is always more crowded

than we perceive it to be.

Remind yourself that each person

around you is protected and loved

by at least one being you can't see.

Alarm Bells

Fall had settled over the community in a blaze of glory: maples, oaks with their purplish-brown leaves, the hawthorns with red berries clumped at the end of the branches.

It may have been the dry summer or the dusty, dry fall now under way that unleashed all the germs early, but it was the worst flu season in memory. Newscasters were predicting one of the worst winters for illnesses.

It had hit Sara the week before Halloween.

She had been sidelined for two days with a headache, cough, and fever. Finally she had gone to the doctor, who, while he sympathized, was himself sneezing up a storm. He sent her home with pills and potions that "knocked her out," as she put it.

"At least while you're sleeping, you won't be coughing," said her husband sympathetically, pulling on his work gloves and hunting for the matches. "You rest," he advised. There was very little wind that day, and he was going out to rake and burn the leaves while she slept. "When I come in, I'll fix you a nice supper," he promised.

Sara smiled to herself as she lay down on the couch, pulling the quilt up to her chin. Her husband's idea of fixing a nice supper was opening a can of soup, heating the contents, and serving it on a tray with crackers arranged around the soup bowl like sunflower petals! But at least he was thoughtful and caring. That's what gave the soup he offered that special taste, that little extra something.

For 35 years he had been doing just such thoughtful things. She was a fortunate lady, if you believed half the tales you saw on TV or read in magazines. Or, she had to admit sadly, even if she listened to some of her friends.

Succumbing to the medicine's pull, she drifted off into a deep, drug-induced slumber with a smile on her face thinking of this special man put-

tering in the backyard with his rake and wagon. He loved being busy. Retirement had not slowed him down a bit; it just gave him more time to think up projects to accomplish.

Sara was sound asleep when someone started pounding on her back door. Groggily, she got to her feet. "I'm coming," she called, pulling on her bathrobe. In her confused haste, Sara tripped over the quilt. She gathered it in her arms to avoid falling.

"Hurry!" shouted the person at the door.

When she opened it, however, there was no one there... only her husband out by the road burning leaves in the ditch. As she watched, he lost his balance and fell into the flames.

He couldn't get up.

It was as if Sara's bathrobe had wings. She got to the fire in time to pull him to safety and wrap him in the quilt she had been dragging.

"No," he told her later at the hospital, "I didn't see anybody in the yard or on the porch coming to get you. It was just my lucky day that you woke up when you did."

They held hands... until the nurse brought him his supper: Soup that Sara fed him, after she blessed it with a prayer for its nourishment and with a thank-you to the angel who had given her more time with her husband here on earth.

Torrey: Airedale or Angel?

Having my own dog made me feel safe, especially when my husband was out of town or working late, which he had to do quite often. My dog, Torrey, was a lovable, playful, sometimes hardheaded Airedale terrier, who was good for my soul and my sanity.

We lived in a suburb of Washington, D.C. Since I'd brought Torrey home as a puppy five years earlier, I worried less and less about the muggers and other criminals I heard about on the nightly local news. But what endeared Torrey to me even more was the way she had gracefully given up her favored position as my "baby" when I was fortunate enough to have a real baby a few years ago. Torrey was a true-blue member of our family who stayed by my side when she wasn't keeping me busy opening the door for her to go outside or to come back in, dozens of times a day.

"You cater to that dog more than you do me," my husband would tease.

"Well," I'd tease him right back, "she loves me so much she follows me around!"

My husband thought Torrey was a sweet dog, but he was skeptical that she had any value as a watchdog.

"Look how she wags her tail and licks the hand of every stranger she meets," he often reminded me.

"But she's never had any reason to defend us," I'd point out. While I defended her, I'd hoped ardently that we'd never have occasion to find out for sure if she was capable of protecting us.

My husband was working late one March evening, however, when Torrey got her chance. I was getting our daughter ready for bed, and we were playing on the rug beside her crib when I noticed that Torrey had been barking for some time out on the deck. We, like our neighbors, had shut our windows against the early spring chill. Torrey knew she was not allowed to bark endlessly. When she did need to voice an opinion, it was usually a short series of businesslike barks aimed at a squirrel or passing cat, just to let it know who was boss and that it had better mind its manners and stay out of her yard. But these barks drew my attention because they did not stop and because they sounded urgent. I put my daughter in her crib and went out on the deck.

From Torrey's aggressive posture and almost frantic barking, I half-expected to see a strange man standing threateningly in our yard. But there was no one, and I sighed with relief. Yet Torrey continued to bark intensely, so I stayed outside to see if I could find anything wrong.

The neighborhood where we lived was an old one, with large oaks, magnolias, and maples, many of which rose over a hundred feet to form a canopy high over our heads. Our yard was long and narrow and filled with old-growth trees, and behind our fence was an overgrown acre or two that gave us space, privacy, and a screen of natural beauty between our house on Willow and the other neighbors behind us on Maple.

I listened and peered out into the dusky spring evening. It was alive with the sounds of insects and cars passing on neighboring streets. But nothing else. Just as I was turning to go inside, I heard what could have been a shout.

I listened intently. "Well, Torrey, it's probably just some teenagers fooling around over on Maple." But the dog was not pacified; she continued to bark. As I listened further, I thought I heard a faint, almost indistinguishable call for help.

I looked at the backs of the houses over on Maple—they all had inside lights on and windows tightly shut. I wondered if the shout might be from a family argument in one of those houses. If so, I wondered, what should I do?

Then, I heard it clearly—"Help me!"—followed by a muffled cry of pain. I felt the hair on my neck stand up.

Was someone being mugged in the overgrown area behind our yard?

I heard another faint cry, which was cut off abruptly, and then I was certain. Fearing that the attacker might have a knife or gun, I knew I did not have a moment to spare. I grabbed the phone, which was just inside the door, and dialed 911 as I stepped back out to the deck with the phone to my ear.

Without thinking, I yelled as loudly as I could, "Hold on! I'm calling the police!" I was hoping, I guess, that the attacker would stop the attack and run. Torrey continued to bark ferociously, doing her best to help drive the attacker away. The police station was about four blocks from our house, and I hoped it wouldn't take them long to arrive.

The twilight had faded into dusk, and my outside light came on, illuminating me as I stood on the deck talking to the police. I suddenly realized that if the attacker looked my way, he would see clearly that I was the one who had shouted the threat and called the police. I stepped back quickly into the shadows of the house, and I called Torrey urgently to my side.

The police siren sounded while I was still talking to the police. At the moment I heard it, I also heard a noise and looked out to see a man crash into my chain-link fence. He banged into another fence before he found the path a few houses away, and he escaped onto the street. I ran to the front window and saw the man limping away up the street. I was still holding the telephone to my

ear and was still connected to the police, so I hurriedly told the dispatcher what I'd just seen.

A few minutes later I saw two uniformed officers running up the street in the same direction.

Suddenly, I was afraid for my daughter and myself, and I ran around the house locking doors and windows. I closed all the shades and curtains and turned on all the lights. I berated myself for being so stupid as to step out in plain sight and call attention to myself. I hugged Torrey closely and sat outside my daughter's room while I called my husband at work. When I told him what had happened, he left for home at once.

Two hours later, the police came by to get my report. They told us they had apprehended the suspect, and they filled us in on what had taken place. The victim had been walking home on Maple from the metro station when a man stepped out of the bushes and grabbed her. He was very violent and threatened the woman with a gun. The attack took place practically in the backyards of the houses on Maple, but, because everyone's windows were closed, no one had heard the woman's shouts.

No one but Torrey, who had refused to quit trying until she had made someone aware of the danger. The poor woman had suffered a broken jaw, but, thanks to a four-legged guardian angel who would not give up, the attack was stopped and the woman's life was probably saved.

I never dreamed that in addition to keeping our family safe, Torrey would also save the life of a total stranger.

Even my skeptical husband has to agree, "What a dog!" Or is she really an angel in a dog disguise?

Who Were Those Men?

*P*am's stomach tightened, knotted up, and she thought she might be sick. This couldn't be happening. When she had pulled up to a stop sign in a bad part of town, the engine of her car just quit. Desperately she tried starting it again and again, but all she heard was a weak grinding noise, then nothing at all.

She never should have come this way, not by herself and not so late in the day. It was almost nightfall. The sky was getting darker and darker by the moment. She'd never felt so alone in her life. She should at least have carried her phone with her instead of leaving it at work on her desk. How could she have been so careless, so stupid?

Her brain raced frantically. She must do something and do it fast. She didn't want to find herself stranded in a rough part of town, alone, in total darkness. She glanced quickly out the car window, worried what she might see, but there was no one in sight.

Pam shuddered and searched for options. She could sit here in the car and wait, hoping someone would come help her. Maybe her family would start worrying and come hunting for her. But that could take a while. They'd probably think she'd stopped to do a few errands on the way home.

She could leave the car and find a public phone, but the odds of finding one unbroken might be low. Plus, she hated the thought of wandering around in an unfamiliar area as the sky darkened. That would probably be stupid. She could lift the car hood and take a look. Maybe it was something simple, something she could handle herself. But she almost laughed at that idea. She knew as much about cars as she did about brain surgery—absolutely nothing.

Just as she was deciding to leave the car and head for what looked to be a school of some kind, she caught sight of movement from the corner of her eye. From around the side of a huge brick building spilled a loud, boisterous gang of young men, bumping each other, joking and laughing among themselves. Their baggy clothing and hip-hop style frightened her—she knew they were up to no good. Her heart sped up when she spotted them. What should she do now?

She wanted to dash for safety. But where would she run? What could she do now? Maybe if she sat very still, they might not notice her. They might keep walking and never catch sight of her. But no such luck. The entire group of young men turned in her direction, pointing and talking to each other. As her heart slammed inside her chest, she prayed frantically, looking in all directions for help. If she screamed, would anyone hear her or would they even come if they did?

Then the group surrounded her car, leaning close, their faces almost against the car windows.

"Lady?" one youth called through the glass. Pam wanted to just vanish. "You got a problem, ma'am?"

One of the youths had already lifted the hood and peered inside. "Hey, here's the trouble," he called, and the young men all gathered close, a few reaching in to tinker with her car. One leaned around the hood to call to her, "OK, try it now. You had a loose connection here."

She flipped the key and felt a welcome burst of relief as the engine roared to life again.

"This will hold it until you get home, ma'am," one youth explained through the window. "But get it fixed soon, so you won't have problems again."

Only then did she notice that each young man clutched a book. Every single one carried a Bible. She rolled down her window.

"Oh, thank you so much," she told them, feeling wave after wave of relief roll through her. "If you hadn't come along to help, I don't know what I would have done. How can I repay you?"

"Oh, no thanks, ma'am," one told her, his grin wide and full of kindness, which she now noticed when she looked more closely at his face. All their faces were full of kindness. "We were just on our way home from the homeless shelter. We lead a Bible study a couple nights a week down there. We're just glad we could help. And hey, next time somebody needs some help, think of us and pass it on, OK?"

She grinned up into their faces, wondering how she could ever have feared them. She nodded vigorously, "Oh, yes, I sure will. God bless you all. You've been my saving angels tonight for certain."

Then her young angel gang took off down the street, laughing, poking one another, waving over their shoulders at her.

Not only did they fix her car that night, but they also fixed her attitude. She would no longer assume that every group of young men, no matter their color or clothing style, was dangerous. These young men were her guardian angels, but they also warned her about the dangers of making judgments about people until you knew them. She felt blessed by her experience, and she vowed to keep this lesson in her heart forever. She would never forget her angels!

Still Small Voice

The rain started around six. I didn't think much about it at the time. Mountain folks like me are used to the brief thunderstorms that are a common occurrence in the Colorado Rockies. Bob had taken the kids into town to do some shopping after supper. I relished the solitude. You don't get much of it when you have three preschoolers.

Though there were dishes to wash and chores to do, I curled up in the big comfy chair by the front window that overlooks the Big Thompson River. I'd been reading a mystery novel and couldn't wait to get back to it. I was soon so engrossed that the intermittent crashes of thunder and flashes of lightning seemed like part of the story.

Darkness settled in early, and I got up to turn on the lights. Then I glimpsed the road through the driving rain; water was rushing down it. I hoped Bob wasn't coming back through the storm. He'd have trouble seeing the yellow lines on the twisty narrow road. Flash floods, fed by mountain cloudbursts, occur from time to time in the mountains. Folks usually wait them out. I hoped that Bob would buy the kids an ice cream and hang around in town for a while.

I went back to my book, this time more to mask the concern I was feeling than to find out the story's murderer. I couldn't concentrate. Perhaps, I thought, there would be some information about the storm on the radio. When I got up to turn it on, I looked through the darkness at the river in front of me. It had risen some, but I was less worried about the river than the road. I fiddled with the dials looking for a local station that would have news of the storm. There wasn't much. The commentator mentioned high water, but there were no flood warnings yet.

I decided I might as well get the dishes done. There was no avoiding them, and work might keep my mind off my family. I dreaded the thought that they might be driving up through "The Narrows." Surely the road would be covered with water there, and driving would be treacherous.

I still hadn't begun to worry about my own safety. Our house, after all, was well above the river.

The phone rang, and I rushed to get it, hoping it was Bob. I'd tell him to just stay the night with cousins in town. No sense risking getting stranded in the car with three little kids.

It wasn't Bob. I recognized Kenny, our closest neighbor downstream. It was the bridge in front of his house that my family would have to cross to get to our cabin. "It's giving way," he warned. "Don't try to go over it."

Terrified by the implication of his words, I explained that Bob might be approaching the bridge.

"I wouldn't worry," said Kenny. "I heard that the sheriff's not letting anyone start up into the canyon. Guess we're lucky not to live down by the bottom of the river. We'd be looking at a lot of water damage."

As I started to respond, the phone went dead and all the lights in the house went off. I opened the back door to check for lights in neighboring houses. The world was inky black. The wind blew eerily. The angry river hissed.

Looking back over the road we've traveled, we sometimes see our angels more clearly than ever.

Slamming the door shut, I moved hastily through the darkness to grab my coat and the flashlight. If Bob and the kids were already in the canyon, I knew I'd have to warn them not to use the bridge.

The flashlight wasn't much help as I stumbled down the hill toward the river. Torrents of rain drenched me. Dripping hair covered my eyes, so I wasn't sure at first whether the wave of water crashing down the canyon was real. It tore the bridge from its concrete foundation and sent it careening downstream.

I hurried back in the direction of the house. At least I'd be safe there. If Bob did try to come home, he'd see that the bridge was out.

Already I was cold. It would be good to be inside. I'd light the fire we always kept laid in the fireplace and warm up beside it.

I'd just reached the door when I heard a sound...a sound like a child sobbing. It came from above me on the hill. I listened intently. It wasn't the crying of any of my own little ones...a mom can tell her child's cry. I tried to persuade myself that it was an animal, perhaps a stranded bobcat. I wanted to get in out of the cold rain, but when the sound came again, I couldn't ignore it. What if a terrified toddler was really up there, lost and alone, in the pounding rain?

I began climbing slowly and carefully toward the spot where the sound seemed to have come. The jagged rocks were slippery and tore through my jeans when I fell. This is really foolish, I told myself. There can't be a child out here. I aimed my flashlight upward. Nothing! I was ready to turn back when I heard the crying sound again. I continued upward, until, utterly exhausted, I reached the top of the mountain behind our cabin.

The wind had abated slightly, and I no longer heard the crying. Maybe they were one and the same. I wasn't sure, but I was too tired to care. I did not dare climb down. I'd probably break a leg on the descent in the darkness. I shone the flashlight on my watch: 1:30 A.M. The rain would most certainly stop by morning, and I'd be able to see a way to get safely back to our house.

I huddled in a small niche in the boulders and slept intermittently. The sound of churning helicopter blades woke me. A rope ladder was being lowered through the murky sky above.

A man then motioned to me to climb it. Like an obedient child, I did. Strong hands pulled me into the chopper, and then the pilot lifted the helicopter. Voices couldn't be heard over the noise of the blades, so I couldn't ask why I'd been plucked from the mountain. But as soon as I looked down, I knew. The rampaging river had raced down the canyon, carrying with it everything in its path.

Trees and power lines had fallen prey to its force. Bridges and buildings were dragged downstream and deposited in jumbled masses. The helicopter hovered, and I looked in horror at the spot where our house had stood. Part of the chimney was all that remained. If I had been inside I would have died in the devastation. I could only pray that my family had not come home after I headed up the mountain.

When the helicopter landed on the Loveland High School football field, I followed a Red Cross worker into the gym. People milled everywhere. A few large portable chalkboards listed the names of missing people. I saw mine. I didn't see Bob's or the children's—I breathed a sigh of relief. They must be safe.

As I stood figuring out how to contact him, Bob's strong arms encircled me. His eyes were moist. "Thank God you're safe. How did you know to get to higher ground?"

I told him about the crying I'd heard, and I reminded him of the Bible verse that says, "a little child shall lead you." I knew without a doubt that God had sent a little child to lead me.

Guarding Jeremy

"Mom, don't put my socks in that drawer," urged my young daughter as we tackled straightening up her room. We'd turned the task into a fun, together time, pausing for a quick tickle or an exchange of knock-knock jokes. Scooping up discarded clothes from the floor and tidying messy drawers, retucking bed sheets and dust mopping under the bed kept us busily occupied.

Just another normal, noisy, hectic afternoon in a household with small children. Never a quiet moment unless both the kids were sound asleep. My husband was off somewhere doing his share of chores. Our younger child, Jeremy, was contentedly playing in his crib, ready to doze off any moment. I'd checked on him, and he was fine. No problem.

In the other room the radio churned out cheery background music, tunes to clean by. We could hear traffic noises outside, plus the regular neighborhood sounds of dogs barking, people calling to one another, birds chirping. Nothing out of the ordinary.

My daughter and I were enjoying our task, both down on our knees, peering under the bed to check for any stray dust bunnies we had missed. We were talking and laughing, sharing our day's activities, planning what we'd do tomorrow. We were proud of how nice her room was looking. We promised ourselves juice and cookies as a reward for so much hard work.

"Here's another book, Mom," my daughter said, handing me one we'd missed while rearranging her shelves.

I reached for the book, and then, in an instant, I whipped around and dashed from the room. There was nothing that I could say triggered my reaction. In our busy, noisy, bustling household, I hadn't caught some rustle to alert my instinctive parental warning system. Before I had time to think, to wonder what caused me to react, I was up and out of the room, down the hall, moving with swift urgency. My heart was slamming rapidly in my chest.

"Mom?" my daughter called, startled by my sudden dash from the room. "What's wrong?"

I couldn't answer. My brain wasn't even working. I felt as if my mind hadn't caught up with my body. I was moving without thought, without awareness, without plan or purpose.

Down the hall in a flash, I reached for and snatched my small son, crawling across the floor. I scooped him up in my arms, held him close, and felt my heart crashing against my ribs. Somehow he'd climbed from his crib, and pushed open the bedroom door that I thought I had shut firmly. Jeremy was off in search of his dad.

I stood there, holding him, staring straight ahead—through the open basement door, which we always kept closed and latched to prevent accidents. I peered down over the edge, down to the concrete floor in the darkness. I felt panic clutch at me. What if I hadn't moved instantly? I shuddered, thinking of what surely would have happened. My small son would have toppled headlong down

those stairs. I held him even closer, cuddling his warm, precious body in my arms. I pushed the basement door firmly shut with my hip.

I pressed my cheek against his soft, tousled curls, and I began shaking all over. How had I known? What had caused me to move so swiftly and suddenly? What had warned me in time to save my little son's life? It was as if something or someone had yanked me to my feet and pushed me down that hallway. Someone or something had known the terrible danger and shoved me into life-saving action.

We'll never know for sure what triggered my actions. But I can't help thinking there was a watchful angel beside me that day, nudging me out the door and down the hall just in time to save Jeremy's life.

That's what I believe. It's what I'll always believe. And I will be forever grateful.

Perhaps we find it easier to see angels as cute and cuddly, but we should always remember their strength and fierce devotion to us.

Healing Angels

In your deepest distress you

are often covered by angels'

wings on every side.

Trust in Hand

Reaching across the thick hose of the ventilator, my hand found Kyle's where it lay pale and still. Deep, blood-rusty gouges remained where the pavement had chiseled his knuckles. I gently traced each finger.

I remembered counting delicate newborn fingers the first time Kyle was placed in my arms.

I remembered tapping those same fingers with a firm "no-no" when he reached for the top of the stove.

I remembered holding his hand across busy streets.

I remembered teaching him to fold his hands in prayer.

When had his hands grown broad? Manly? *Hairy?*

I peered closer. When was the last time I'd seen his fingernails this clean? Without dirt, axle grease, and house paint?

"It's time to take him down," said Ling, Kyle's nurse of the day. "You'll need to wait outside."

Stroking his arm one last time, I kissed his hot, dry forehead.

"I love you, Sweetie."

Outside the closed Trauma Unit doors, I leaned wearily against the concrete wall. The doctor had ordered another CT scan to investigate spinal cord injuries and to recheck the hemorrhages and swelling in Kyle's brain. My son had been in a coma since the hit-and-run accident days earlier.

God, please, please let things be all right.

I sighed, knowing it would take 30 to 45 minutes for the staff to mobilize the life supports and prepare Kyle for the journey on the elevator. If only I could do something, anything, but wait.

Unmindful and uncaring about the filth of the well-traveled hallway, I slid down and sat on the cold, gritty floor.

And I thought about other hands.

I thought about my husband's. His hands that had held my own so tightly throughout this ordeal.

I thought about the hands of family, friends, and even strangers being folded in fervent, prayerful pleas on our behalf.

I thought about the competent, trained—but impersonal—hands of emergency personnel and those of the nurses, doctors, and technicians working to save Kyle's life. My head sagged against my bent knees.

God, thank you for all those who are serving us and supporting us through this. But this is so big and I feel so small, so incapable, so powerless to help Kyle.

If only I could be in control.

It was hard to place my trust in these strangers. People who didn't know my son. People who didn't love him. It was hard to let others make decisions—big decisions. Life and death decisions.

Help me, God. Please.

The double doors flew open and so did my eyes.

Out swept an entire team of health-care professionals hurrying, pushing Kyle's gurney. From my position on the floor, I saw a fleet of feet moving forcefully, purposefully. I rose to my own. It was then I saw the hands.

Lots of hands. Wheeling, pushing, and carrying. Tending hands. Guiding, adjusting, and straightening. Pairs of hands. . . .

But one pair in particular caught my eye—confident, muscular hands. I didn't see whom they belonged to; I only noticed what they did.

Those hands held a rubber bulb—squeezing it, pressing it. With every firm compression, thick corded veins bulged on the back of each fist. Precisely, strongly, and rhythmically those faithful fingers pumped to a cadence heard only by them.

I gasped in recognition.

The bulb was actually a portable ventilator.

Horrified, I realized those particular hands were manually "breathing" life into Kyle's lungs.

And at that very moment, cold, clear reality smacked me in the face.

As much as I wanted to be, I knew I was not in control; I could not be in control. I could not be my son's caretaker. Simply, Kyle's life was not in *my* hands. There was no choice: I had to let go, to trust.

But I knew wholeheartedly where to place my trust.

Like Job once did, I cried out in all my anguish to God. To God in "whose hand is the soul of every living thing." I knew who held and nurtured Kyle.

The very One "who hath measured the waters in the hollow of his hand" watched over and cared for my son.

I knew he had blessed me with tangible evidence: the life-giving hands of an unknown trauma nurse. One of an army of earth-bound angels. An angel to serve and save another of his cherished children. An angel placed precisely, purposely in the here and now. An angel of our very own.

With hands together and fingers tucked under my chin, I wandered down the hollow hospital hallway, finally willing to let go. Kyle wouldn't be alone. I knew that someone greater, surer than me cradled my precious son.

And, like the psalmist, I prayerfully uttered, "My times are in thy hand."

You can see part of an angel's world in the peace of a sleeping child.

Wrapped in Love

There was really no reason for Nadine to feel as bad as she did, but that was the worst thing about suffering from depression. Often your life could look so perfect on the outside but be a total disaster inside, where it counted. Nadine's life was like that. She was attractive and successful at her job as a nurse practitioner, and she had several good friends she could always count on.

But none of these things mattered once the depression hit. When it hit, it hit hard and sent Nadine reeling. Life became nothing more than a struggle just to get out of bed every morning.

Depression was a disease she had suffered from for years; she had tried every remedy known to medical science, including most of the anti-depressants on the market. None had worked, and many had made her feel worse. She had dieted, exercised, and tried yoga, and she would often feel better for a short time, only to be overcome by the thick fog that would eventually catch up with her.

As a nurse practitioner, she knew a lot about clinical depression, yet even she couldn't seem to find a "cure." She was left feeling empty, and nothing on the face of the earth could fill the void within her.

When Nadine's mother died after a long battle with breast cancer, the darkness became all-pervasive, and Nadine found it almost impossible to get through each day without great physical and emotional effort. She consulted her doctor and was given a powerful sedative to help her get through the next few weeks, but Nadine hated the way the drug made her feel even more sluggish and deadened. She wanted to feel alive, not numb and robotic. She felt at the end of her rope and had to miss two weeks of work, which had once been a place of comfort for her. Getting lost in helping others helped her feel better, too.

Knowing that she desperately needed help, Nadine called a good friend, Carrie, who had always been able to give Nadine perspective and hope with wise advice and gentle humor. Carrie wasn't home, and Nadine was hesitant to leave a message on the machine, so she hung up. She felt so alone, as though the walls of the world were closing in on her. She thought about the pills her doctor had given her and how easy it would be to take them all and surrender to a peaceful sleep free of torment. The thought of taking her own life woke her up enough to realize she had to get out of the house before she did something that could not be undone.

Nadine got in her car and drove. She was going in circles, confused and in tears. This had to stop, she thought, for she didn't think she could take another day of waking up to depression. She took a sudden right-hand turn into a small parking lot just a few blocks from her house. She found herself stopping the car in front of a tiny church tucked away from the street.

As she got out of the car, Nadine jumped, startled, as her car door slammed shut without her touching it. She stared at it a moment, then turned toward the church. She walked in, something she would never have done before; it was a denomination she was unfamiliar with. But that didn't matter, she just needed somewhere quiet and safe to sit and get her head together. A church was the perfect place.

Even more perfect was the fact that the small, quaint church was empty. Nadine entered the lovely sanctuary and sat in a pew in the shadows. She sighed and felt some of the pressure release from her tired shoul-

ders. In the dim candlelit room, she sensed a peace she had never found outside its walls. The tears deep inside her rose to the surface. For almost an hour, Nadine cried freely, letting all the pent-up emotion and pain slip away. When she had no more tears, she clasped her hands together and prayed quietly, head bowed and eyes closed.

She prayed for inner peace, for the hope that God would help lift her out of the darkness. She prayed for serenity, and, as she did, a warmth enveloped her and she felt someone lovingly and gently embrace her. Startled, Nadine raised her head and opened her eyes, expecting to see a priest or nun or someone kind and caring standing over her. But no one was there; the church was empty! Her arms tingled with goose bumps; she *had* felt someone holding her, but who? She sat there basking in the warmth of a love she had never felt before, a love that now swelled from within until it overflowed from her.

The feeling of being embraced returned, and Nadine sat and let the feeling wash over her like healing waters. She was being held, and her body began to rock back and forth, gently, soothingly. Nadine knew that something within her was changing, and that what she had been missing from her life had now been found. In all her years fighting depression, she had been looking for a cure from the outside when it was her inner spirit that longed to be acknowledged and healed. She felt so light, so free, that she started to laugh.

Had someone walked into the church just then, they would have been surprised to see a woman, laughing and smiling, sitting in the back pew surrounded by a glowing white light, with her eyes closed and her face turned up as if viewing something inspiring. But what Nadine saw wasn't visible; it was the love of God that filled her with hope and assurance that this day was the beginning of her journey to healing.

With the help of God, and her angel, Nadine knew that this time she would win her battle with depression. She would know, for the first time in years, what it was to live a life free of pain and emptiness. The void that had haunted her would now be filled with joy.

Angels never doubt the omnipotent power of good.

Falcon Spirit at Medicine Wheel

Here I am, 35 years old and healthy, walking in the Big Horn Mountains of Wyoming. The scenery here is nothing short of breathtaking. I look like a woman alone on vacation, and this is what I told my friends and family back East that I would be doing. But, in truth, I'm not on vacation—I'm running away from home, or what little is left of my home after my trusted soul mate let his midlife crisis ruin our life together. That was more than a year ago, yet I still reel from the shock, anguish, anger, and betrayal. Bitterness seems to be taking over my life.

I'm feeling sorry for myself, I know. But until last fall, I was happy, in love with my husband of ten years, and securely employed at a useful job. We'd just finished building our dream house, and I'd seen my future stretching into a peaceful life, hoping there would be children, even grandchildren. But that dream is shattered, and I find myself staring at a future as empty and frightening as the space on the other side of that cliff, where the ground drops off so abruptly that I'm afraid to even go close enough to peer over to see what's at the bottom.

Our newly built house remains intact, mocking me with the absurdity of my expectations, with the ghosts of memories that will never be. "Face the facts," a friend told me last month, "it's over with Eddie. But now you're free, free to go anywhere, do anything—see it as a new chance. A fresh start," she said.

She's right, I know, but I feel paralyzed with fear, the same way I'm afraid to venture too close to the edge of the cliff. One thing I've always wanted to do, I'd admitted to her, was to live out here, in the West, where you can see mountains and wildlife and feel like you have room to breathe.

"Well, go out there," she encouraged. "Check it out, and see if you can find work."

So I've been here for a week, driving around, looking in the paper for jobs. I've circled some that look promising but have yet to call about any—that would make it all too real.

This morning I decided to take a long walk in the mountains to clear my head. I decided to visit the ancient Medicine Wheel that the innkeeper said was out at the end of this long ridge. According to him, until some-one spotted it from a plane a few decades ago, its only visitors for maybe a thousand years were the falcons, eagles, mountain goats, and other wild creatures that frequent such high, windy places. No one knows what hap-pened to the people who worshiped here in ancient times; I picture these mysteriously vanished people as an early Indian culture where the high priests and priestesses kept vigil at the highest place around to better com-mune with the spirits.

At 10,000 feet, I'm hiking in the clouds. Beside me the land drops sharply and, though it is August, a layer of old snow still covers slopes where boulders block the sun. The wet snow makes some sections of the path treacherous, and I suddenly wonder if it's safe to be out here alone. What if the path slips out from under me and I go barreling, crashing down the slope? I'm angry all over again at my ex-husband for this predicament—

Heavenly ears hear you and rush to touch you with love.

shouldn't he be here to hold my hand, prevent my fall? I think about giving up and turning back. But then I recognize that doing so would only add to my feelings of failure, bitterness, and unworthiness. As I stand here, too frightened to move, I suddenly realize that this high mountain ridge where I stand, and the abyss all around, embody my fears about the future.

A cry comes from above: a peregrine falcon. It tucks its wings and dives like a missile, disappearing behind the ridge. I've always been attracted to these fearless raptors who embody beauty, fierceness, and speed. I'm excited to see one so near. It's a large female, and her white chest and throat stand in beautiful contrast to her pink belly and blue-gray back. I almost forget my fear of the abyss as I'm seized with the desire to scramble over the boulders to see where the falcon went. But I don't know how far I still have to walk, and I'm fearful of detours. A feather floats near me to the ground. I pick it up. A white throat feather—maybe she's telling me something.

The ridge stretches away, my destination ahead somewhere, but hidden from sight. A lot like my life these days: I'm unsure of my destination and fearful, but I'm not turning back! Somehow, for good or ill, I'm on my way.

After the fifth slippery slope, they don't seem nearly so bad. These boots have good soles, I realize, and hey, here I am—by myself—actually making progress!

As I finally reach the high plateau at the end of the ridge, a strong wind rushes past, singing and chilling my ears. I am awestruck by the intense beauty and isolation of this place.

Ahead is the Medicine Wheel. I'm shocked, at first, to see a tall, chain-link fence enclosing it. I'd expected this place to remain wild and untouched, no different now than when the ancient high priests and priestesses disappeared. But soon I ignore the fence as the Medicine Wheel itself draws me closer. This "wheel" is a circle, about 80 feet wide, made of piled rocks. More rocks radiate outward in lines from a central "hub." I count 29 of these "spokes."

The high fence was no doubt put there to keep people from taking the rocks as souvenirs. Or perhaps to hold at bay people like me who have an urge to rebuild the places where the rocks have fallen away. Mountain bluebirds come and go, flitting over the fence and hopping from spoke to spoke. Outside the fence is an expanse of flat rocks—a plaza? These rocks are mysteriously smooth, like tiles in a mosaic laid by the hand of God.

But the fence serves another purpose in this modern world: Tied to it are hundreds of small prayer bundles left in this place of spirits. Ancients built Medicine Wheel, moderns added the fence. Now the fence has become a part of its strong medicine. I was wrong earlier when I said this site is deserted; it is still very much in use.

Impulsively, I reach into my knapsack for pen and paper. The note I scribble says: "Could you give me a sign—should I take this leap of faith?"

The move west would be a challenge for me, a journey into the unknown. I would have only myself to rely on. Back home, at least, I have a job, friends, and family. But I also walk a landscape littered with broken promises, shattered dreams. Could the West, with its wide open spaces, soothe my spirit and allow it, once again, to soar?

I take the falcon's feather and a small rose quartz crystal that I carry in my pocket, and I wrap them with the note in the hanky my mother always told me I'd need. I tie the bundle to the fence. The wind swirls around me, singing louder—or are those actually voices I hear? I step back quickly and look around, but no one is there.

Suddenly, the falcon appears again, seeming to rise directly from the Medicine Wheel. The falcon circles, then drops from the sky to alight on the fence. Oddly, she sits directly above the little bundle I had just tied there. The falcon is beautiful, and amazingly close to me. I can see her eyes, meeting my own with a fierce, commanding look. I note the dark, distinctive mustache stripe as I hold my breath. Then, the bird spreads her wings and swoops toward me, almost touching my feet with a pointed wingtip before soaring upward, high above the ridge. Folding her wings, she plummets, straight into the abyss.

A scream strangles in my throat. But the falcon reappears moments later, wings spread, soaring on thermals, climbing higher and higher. Her cry pierces my heart, and suddenly I know that the falcon is God's messenger, my angel, sent to encourage me to follow my dreams. To tell me that I, too, can trust in the updrafts and let my spirit soar. I spend a long time at the Medicine Wheel, though the peregrine has gone. Angel voices sing all around me, and the feeling of spirituality is strong; it is a force that flows from this high place of rock, wind, and sky. Winged creatures keep their vigil above the grand contours of the land at this holy place.

I walk back on the spine of this upswept ridge feeling lighter, buoyed by updrafts playing constantly around me. They caress my folded wings and taunt them to open wide, to bear me higher in ever-spiraling ascent, until finally, with my falcon's steady gaze, I plummet, straight for my target.

And I seize the prize in my talons and make it mine.

May Day

Time. There's just too much of it in here.

Yet, Brenda could remember when she seemed to never have enough time. Of course that was before, when she had bustled through the full days and nights of motherhood and normalcy. The comparison—of then and now—suddenly gave new meaning to the phrase, "Once upon a *time!*"

And I'm sick and tired of being on a schedule.

Schedule, not routine. Routine was different. Routine meant fixing breakfast in the morning. Routine meant giving her husband a kiss along with his sack lunch each day. Routine meant doing laundry every Monday. A schedule, on the other hand, was something you stuck with because you had to. Like being bathed each morning at 10:00. Being turned three times each shift to prevent bedsores. Or even being diapered—as regular as clockwork—every time you were, well, *regular*.

Brenda groaned inwardly at her clever play on words, something she'd always been good at. *I AM good at. It's something—the one thing—I am STILL good at. In fact, God, people used to admire me for my quick wit.*

And she still had it. Only, no one knew but her. Even now, like this, she was something more than IV feedings, more than a nurse's duty, more than a wasted body. Did anyone remember that? Did God?

Are you listening God? Or can't you hear me think over the hum of this respirator?

Why, Brenda could hardly hear herself think. The rhythmic hiss and underlying drone of the oxygen muffled each and every sound. It insulated her. Irritated her. Isolated her.

I despise being so helpless.

That's what the advanced stages of MS had done. It was a demon that stripped you of both your dignity and your choices. Like a thief in the night, multiple sclerosis sneaked in to rob you of one treasure after another: sensation, dexterity, range of motion, coordination, strength. Now, at 53, she found herself as helpless as a baby—worse, even. At least an infant had a voice to indicate its needs.

I miss so much.

Brenda could remember (after all, she had lots and lots of time to remember) her favorite activity: traipsing through the woods after a fresh rain. She recalled how it made the soil cocoa-rich and how the breeze was as crisp and clean as a new dollar bill. She loved how the rain left everything smelling as sweet as a freshly bathed baby.

I feel so deserted, God. So alone. I'm not certain you're even there anymore. Are you, God? Are you there?

In the waning evening light, Brenda let her gaze slide around her room at Front Range Manor.

She focused on the wall-to-wall photos tacked up by good-hearted, well-meaning friends and family. On days like today, the pictures were bullet-sharp reminders of a life she didn't-have-couldn't-have-wouldn't-have.

Plump tears bounced their way down her cheeks, and she was too helpless even to wipe them away. She closed her eyes.

"Brenda," hesitantly.

"Brenda," louder.

"Brenda, are you awake?"

Brenda tediously twisted her mouth into a guttural answer. "Wha...aaa...ahh."

"Today is the first of May, Brenda. May Day, and I wanted to share it with you. Here, smell."

Even with her eyes closed, Brenda recognized the springtime scent of lilacs tickling her nose. Mmm, lilacs. They even *smelled* purple; they brought back pleasant memories of her Grandma Belle. Yes, little Grandma Belle, who smelled like talcum powder and always dressed in shades of violet.

"And feel this. It's from the park across the street. The blue jay's loss but our gain," the clear voice tinkled.

Powder soft, a feather stroked—delicately, deliberately—across her forehead, dallied down her cheek, and on to her chin. Meandering over folds in her neck and into nooks behind her earlobes, the downy quill discovered a new path and traced it lazily up the other side of her face. Then, a playful swipe to her nose, like dotting an "i," and the feather was gone.

"Oh, and Brenda, what would spring be without its sounds!"

Magically, the chirping of birds filled and flooded both her ears and her room. The music was light and airy. The simple melody flowed from engaging to majestic and on to joyous. She could almost see the birds climbing and dipping and winging their way across the sky. Twittering, trilling, thrilling her with sweetness and filling her with the goodness of life.

So, this is what it feels like to be ministered to by an angel. By someone who knows me. The inner me. Thank you, Father, thank you.

A smile stole across Brenda's face, crinkling the corners of her closed eyes, tweaking the edges of her mouth, and sneaking onto her parted lips.

Brenda didn't see the new volunteer slip out of her room.

Brenda didn't hear the door whisper shut.

Brenda didn't feel alone.

The cassette player still warbled. The oxygen pulsed on.

Compound Interest

Angels have visited humanity by streams and in deserts, by cradles and by graves, and by altars and by bedsides. Angels have touched us at the most earthly of places, but they have seldom left us the same way they found us.

Few people ever suspected that Sue Ellen had a problem. She juggled her roles as wife to Phil, mother to Harlan and Katy, and her at-home job as a magazine writer so successfully that people called her a regular Martha Stewart.

"It's not a problem," Sue Ellen had said when her husband sat her down one evening and asked her about her drinking. "Maybe I have been having a few more drinks lately," she admitted, "but life's been kind of hectic, what with the move, Dad's heart attack, and all the time you've had to spend traveling for work. Besides," she'd continued defensively, "I can stop any time I want to. Remember last year, I didn't have a single drink during Lent."

Phil had patted her arm. He'd put off talking to Sue Ellen about the problem for months, maybe years. He loved her despite her drinking and had truly hoped that this moment of reckoning would never come. "Honey," he said, "I'm just worried about you. Tell you what, we just won't keep any liquor in the house. Then you won't be tempted." When Sue Ellen frowned at him, he added tenderly, "I'm not trying to be mean. I'm only doing it because I love you."

Sue Ellen hadn't said anything. She knew it wouldn't be hard to stow away a bottle or two for those times when she really needed a drink.

At Sue Ellen's annual checkup, the doctor noticed the shaking hands and weight loss—signs of alcoholism. He had asked her about her drink-

ing. "Alcohol can cause liver damage," he'd said. "These pamphlets discuss the dangers of excessive drinking and give you the numbers of a local AA contact."

Sue Ellen had politely thanked him for the literature but protested, "Don't worry about me, I just drink socially. I certainly don't have a drinking problem."

A few months later Harlan's preschool teacher asked Sue Ellen to stay for a few minutes after class. Mrs. Murphy had waited until all the other parents left. She'd sent Harlan across the hall on an errand and then asked Sue Ellen to sit down. "It's about the field trip to the farm," she'd said. "I know you volunteered to be a driver, but several of the other mothers have told me that they don't want their children riding in your car. When the moms have chatted with you in the hall, they've noticed that you've smelled like you'd been drinking."

Sue Ellen had been offended.

"I'm only mentioning this because we all care about you," said Mrs. Murphy. "And, of course, we care about the welfare of the children, so we can't let you drive for field trips until you stop drinking."

"It's really none of their business," said Sue Ellen. "Besides I hardly ever drink in the daytime."

"One of our other mothers is in AA," said Mrs. Murphy. "I know she'd be happy to talk with you."

Sue Ellen had declined the offer.

She'd also adamantly declined her mother's offer to come and stay with the children so Sue Ellen could go to a residential treatment facility.

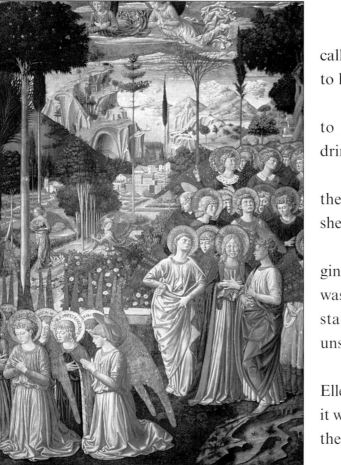

"We're worried about you, dear," her mother said. "Sometimes your words seem a little slurred when we call."

"It's just my allergies," Sue Ellen had reassured her.

On a day the kids didn't have school, Sue Ellen called the mother of one of Katy's friends. "We'd love to have Rachel come over to play."

"I'm sorry, Sue Ellen, but we don't feel you are able to provide adequate supervision when you've been drinking. We'd love to have Katy come here, though."

Sputtering furiously, Sue Ellen had slammed down the phone. "Rachel's mom says you can play there," she'd explained to Katy.

When Katy left, Sue Ellen fixed herself a glass of gin and sat down in the rocker in the living room. She was still there a little later when the doorbell rang. She started to stand to get the door but, being a little unsteady, just called out, "Come on in."

It was Katy's teacher. "What a surprise!" said Sue Ellen. She hadn't said it was a pleasant surprise, because it wasn't. Maybe, she thought, Ms. Steffens would think the gin was just ice water.

Ms. Steffens wasn't fooled. She didn't beat around the bush either.

"I've come here today because I'm worried about Katy. The other children are beginning to talk about your drinking problem, and I'm afraid that soon other mothers won't want their children playing with her if this continues."

Suddenly Sue Ellen was sobbing. "It's already happened. Just today Rachel's mother said she couldn't come over here."

Ms. Steffens spoke soothingly, "I know you love your little ones and you want the best for them. Your drinking is not something you can control yourself. I have a friend in AA. Would you like her to come over?"

Sue Ellen hesitated only a second. "Yes," she said firmly.

Six months later, still sober, Sue Ellen went to school to thank Ms. Steffens. She hugged the older woman and said, "You were an angel to help me face my drinking problem."

Ms. Steffens smiled, "I was just one of the many angels sent to encourage you to seek help. Sometimes it takes a whole heavenly host to get God's message across."

Angels are more than good luck charms or well-wishers.
They are as vital as the lives we strive to live.

Someone to Watch Over You

Angela knew something was terribly wrong when Donny wouldn't respond. She could feel no pulse, and he wasn't breathing, even with her feeble attempts to give him rescue breathing and CPR. The driver of the car that had slammed into them knelt down next to her. He was a young man, with blood all over his face and left arm. He apologized profusely, claiming he had dodged a dog cutting across the freeway. Angela knew he was telling the truth; she had seen the dog lope off to the shoulder, safe and unharmed. But her husband was lying here unconscious, and she was filled with fear and anger.

When the ambulance arrived, Donny was loaded onto a gurney as paramedics began rescue attempts. Angela was helped into the ambulance even though she wasn't injured, and she felt herself go numb as they sped off to Shoreham Emergency and Trauma Center. She hung on to Donny's hand, barely aware that the rescue team had gotten his pulse back and that he was breathing again, albeit with great difficulty.

As the paramedics wheeled Donny into Shoreham, Angela tried to hold onto his hand but lost him in a sea of nurses and doctors rushing to his aid. She heard the words "internal bleeding" and "emergency surgery" over and over, as if echoing in her head, and then a nurse was holding her hand and explaining Donny's grave situation.

Angela was allowed to kiss Donny on the forehead before she watched the staff wheel him off to surgery. She longed to be with him, knowing he would need her there. Deep inside, she knew that she wanted to be there for another reason, too, afraid that if Donny died, it would be her last chance to tell him she loved him. She glanced up one last time as a nurse swung open the ER doors and Donny's gurney rolled down the hallway.

There, at the side of the gurney, holding Donny's hand, was a woman in white. Angela wondered if she was one of the ER nurses, but something was different about this woman. When Angela realized what it was, she blanched. The woman was not in nurse whites, but she wore a flowing white gown. And she floated above the ground as she turned to face Angela. Who is she? Angela wondered, thinking perhaps her panic and exhaustion were causing hallucinations. Had someone slipped her a sedative without her being aware of it? But there the woman was, hovering beside Donny, holding his hand and looking back at Angela with a knowing smile and an understanding nod. As the woman walked through the ER doors, Angela noticed that the nurses and doctors seemed not to see or acknowledge her presence. In fact, they seemed to be walking through her!

At that moment, Angela felt peace. She was overwhelmed with a feeling of tranquility, and she knew that Donny was going to live. But when the noises of the ER room came through the open door, Angela snapped out of her reverie and immediately the fear overtook the sweet calm she had just experienced.

The ER doors slammed shut, and a nurse told Angela that the surgery would take several hours and she could go home. But Angela refused to leave Donny alone. She decided to stay in the waiting room. As she waited, she thought about the woman in white and how much she looked like an

Angels are everyday wonders. They are reminders to us that life is not just what we see and touch, what we define and explain. Life is also invisible friends and protectors from other worlds who stand by us to the end.

angel. This thought stayed in her mind as she drifted off to deep, much-needed sleep.

Five hours later, a doctor in scrubs gently shook Angela awake. It took her a moment to awaken, for she had been having a dream that she

hadn't wanted to end. In her dream, Donny was alive and healthy and whole, and they were standing on a beach together, talking and laughing about the crash as if it had happened in a past lifetime.

She heard the surgeon saying something about Donny's kidney being punctured, and that the delicate surgery had been successful. She hung onto the word "successful" and let the surgeon help her stand up. He told her Donny was in ICU and would be there for at least a week, and that he was still asleep from the surgery. Angela could, however, see him if she wanted to, although the surgeon couldn't promise her that he would be coherent enough to recognize her.

She didn't care, she wanted to see Donny. A few minutes later, Angela walked into the ICU recovery area, where two nurses and a doctor bustled about trying to make her husband comfortable. Donny was not awake, but Angela could see his face and it looked peaceful despite the past few hours. She smiled, knowing how close to death he had been. She turned to ask the attending doctor a question, when she saw her again.

Standing just behind the machines that monitored Donny's heart and lungs was the woman in white. She was looking down at Donny with a loving and protective gaze. The woman slowly looked up and smiled at Angela. Before Angela could smile back, the doctor was talking to her, telling her all about Donny's surgery and how strong and courageous her husband had been.

When the doctor finished informing Angela about the long recovery procedures, she thanked him profusely for saving her husband's life. She almost choked on her breath when the doctor laughed and said, "Well,

I'm not so sure I should get all the credit. I think your husband has a guardian angel up there somewhere. He's going to be just fine."

The doctor's words reverberated over and over in Angela's head as she turned to look at the woman in white. She stood, or rather floated, by the rear ICU doors, gazing back at Angela. Angela smiled and mouthed the words "Thank you." The woman smiled back at her and nodded, the same way she had done when Donny was being wheeled into surgery. And then she vanished through the doors. Angela strained to see through the glass to the hallway on the other side of the doors, but there was no one there.

She thought about running after the woman, wanting to confirm her vision, needing to know if the woman was real or just a figment of a mind so scared and exhausted it would have believed anything. Instead, Angela turned toward the one thing she knew was real, her love for Donny. She went and leaned over him, kissing him softly on his forehead. As she did, he stirred in his sedated slumber and whispered, "Hi, baby." Angela knew that they *were* being watched over and that everything really was going to be all right.

Flying in Formation

Suzanne rested her back against the airplane seat. She was exhausted! The last few days had been the hardest of her life. Her father's death was so unexpected. Sixty-two was too young to die. He'd always said he'd never get old, but everybody knew that he'd really meant he didn't want to end up needing other people to care for him. Not that anyone would have minded.

"Hoot," as everyone called him, was a hoot. He always had a smile, a joke to tell, a trick to play. But it hadn't been his sense of humor that had earned him the nickname. He'd been a wildlife carver who had created wonderfully realistic renditions of birds and waterfowl. How lucky they were to have his carvings as a tangible legacy. Every time she saw the Canada goose in her entryway she'd be reminded of him.

When they were growing up, she and Jake and Micah had spent hours in their dad's studio. They'd battled wood dust when they came in for help with their homework and endured the smell of turpentine when they'd come in to bargain for a later curfew. They'd learned life's lessons amid the ducks and songbirds their dad had spent so much of his free time carving out of wood.

He'd always used bird analogies to explain things. They'd practiced turning their heads like owls so they'd remember to look at problems from all directions. He'd explained how duck hunters used decoys to warn the kids not to be fooled by friends who said drugs wouldn't hurt them. When he was alive, Hoot had hated to hear his children arguing. He'd always encouraged them to work together. "Family is forever," he'd say. He'd remind them of the Canada geese that flew over their summer place in Michigan. "See," he'd say, "how they move in formation. Moving that way makes it easier for all of them to fly."

Suzanne looked out the airplane window. Her eyes misted over as she thought back to the night she'd gotten the call with the news of her dad's death. At least he'd died in his sleep. But none of them had been there.

She and Jake and Micah had flown to Chicago as soon as they'd heard. The first morning they'd huddled, heartbroken, around the kitchen table. Jake had searched Hoot's files for any papers that might help them make final arrangements. He'd found duck patterns and the entry form for the National Carver's Show in Ocean City, Maryland, but no will and nothing about his father's wishes.

"It's obvious that Dad hadn't planned on dying anytime soon," said Jake. There were unpaid bills stuffed in the spice rack, and they couldn't even locate his checkbook.

"First things first," said Micah. "We've got to make the funeral arrangements."

They'd moved out to the deck with their coffee and the bagels one of the neighbors had brought by. Edgy from lack of sleep and overwhelmed by their sense of loss, they'd begun to argue.

Suzanne had been sure Hoot would have wanted to be cremated.

"No way," said Jake.

The argument intensified. "Fine," Suzanne had said. "Do it your way. I'll just fly back to Colorado and let you two make all the decisions." As she'd flounced off, they had heard a strange honking sound overhead.

They'd looked up. A flock of Canada geese in perfect formation was circling above the house.

They'd stared at each other in amazement. Canada geese didn't head down from the upper peninsula until much later in the summer.

Suzanne smiled as she remembered the comment Jake had made. "I didn't realize that angels could disguise themselves as geese."

They hadn't had to translate the honks. They'd gotten the message. Together they had made the rest of the decisions without further dis-agreement.

Suzanne closed her eyes as the plane soared homeward.

A new beginning, like the breath of an angel, makes the air a little sweeter and the world seem full of hope.

Quite an Act

Before Carol entered the hospital for treatment of breast cancer, she had been a very private person, preoccupied with her husband and family. She seldom reached out to strangers.

Treatment of her disease required extensive chemotherapy, first as an inpatient and then as an outpatient. The treatment killed off the cancer, but Carol lost her hair, a thick honey-colored mane that had been her crowning glory. Carol was horrified.

Overcome with relief at the chemo's success, her husband couldn't see what all the fuss was about. "They say it will grow back. Get a wig," he advised.

Carol donned a scarf and headed out with a list of shops that carried wigs. She went through most of them, finding that each store's selection seemed worse than the last. All the wigs looked like, well, wigs! Finally, she found a small shop where the owner urged her to try on a few. Carol had to admit that a couple of the wigs weren't too bad. One looked close enough to her real hair, so she bought it.

On her next trip back to the hospital, the nurses raved over Carol's wig.

"I want you to meet somebody," one of the nurses urged, taking Carol into a patient's room. A pale woman sat up in the bed, her hair gone except for a few wispy strands.

"Carol, this is Elizabeth. You two have a lot in common. Do you mind if I tell, Carol?" the nurse asked.

Something popped in shy Carol, as if a flower were opening inside her. "I'll do better than that," Carol announced, and pulled the wig off with a dramatic flourish.

Elizabeth gasped, and the nurse giggled. "It's great. Where did you get it?" Elizabeth asked, showing a hint of enthusiasm.

"Oh, there are lots of good ones. You just have to try a few. Can I bring some in for you?" Carol asked.

Carol had found her mission. After that, the nurses called whenever a patient was struggling to cope with hair loss. Carol brought sample wigs and blithely did her disappearing hair act. Most times, she and the patient ended up laughing together. When Carol's hair eventually grew back, she carried pictures of herself bald and with her wig.

"It's not just vanity," Carol explained to one patient's husband. "It's part of getting yourself and your life back. No one understands that better than someone who's lived through it."

We do the work of angels when we reach out to someone.

Guardian Angels

One day when we face these beings of light who have guided our paths and done God's work in our lives, we will wonder how we ever overlooked their presence.

Heaven Help Jake

The huge semi barreled up the icy hill toward him. Jake, just 17 and wondering how he could have been caught out in this ice storm, clutched the steering wheel tightly and pumped the brakes of his little coupe as he maneuvered his way slowly downhill, peering ahead into the darkness. Suddenly, he was blinded by the light of the truck's high beams as it hit a patch of ice.

The truck skidded out of control and into Jake's car. The crunching sound of the impact reverberated in the snow-covered night. The semi plowed sideways, out of control, pushing Jake's car in front of it at a sickening speed, until both vehicles were stopped by a mammoth oak tree.

When it was over, Jake was in the ditch with the overturned truck on top of his crushed vehicle.

Barely conscious, Jake realized that he was seriously hurt. There was a deep gash in his side, and his legs were pinned in the wreckage. He thought of how disappointed his dad would be that the car was wrecked. He thought of how his mom would worry. "Help me, please," Jake repeated to himself over and over.

Help wasn't likely. Since he heard no sounds from the truck, he thought the truck driver must also be injured. With the storm raging, there wasn't much traffic. No one saw the wreck, and no one happened upon it.

Jake felt himself slipping into darkness. Then he sensed someone nearby. A voice said, "Hang on. Help is coming." Someone held his hand to keep him from slipping away. A few minutes later, a fire department rescue unit arrived, prying the wreck apart and freeing Jake. An hour later, he was in a hospital emergency room with nurses and doctors all around him.

When he began to recover, he asked everyone if they knew who had helped him. No one knew. Whoever called 911 hadn't left a name, and the dispatcher couldn't find a record of the call. No one was at the scene when the ambulance arrived.

In fact, the fire chief told him, there was no way anyone could have gotten close to him through the wreckage.

Jake thought about taking out a newspaper ad. He was sure if he looked hard enough, he would find the person and thank his mysterious savior. Was it a young man, he wondered, maybe about his own age?

He proposed the idea to this mother. "Somehow, I don't think you'll find the person," she said. "I started praying for you as soon as the ice started. I kept on praying until they called me from the emergency room to tell me you were going to be fine," she went on, wiping tears from her eyes. "Whoever helped you was an answer to prayers. It's clear to me who we need to thank."

"The Grinch" Who Stole Kathy

We called our dog "Max the Grinch" because, like the Dr. Seuss character, he loved to steal things, especially presents from beneath the Christmas tree. When he was a puppy dragging off shoes, toys, throw rugs, books—anything he could get his mouth around—we laughed. The joke wore thin as he grew into a 75-pound hound who was known to have knocked over a large barbeque grill to snatch the steaks and to have intercepted baseballs in the middle of games.

"What are we going to do about that dog?" The exasperated question came more and more often—until one icy winter day when we found out that he was our very own guardian angel.

After a night of freezing rain, we awakened to a landscape encased in crystal. We kids couldn't wait to get outside. Neither, of course, could Max. With all the gleeful cracking icicles falling from the porch railing and landing on the mirror-bright driveway, no one heard the first telltale crack—except Kathy. Just seven years old, Kathy was happily swinging on a rope suspended from a limb of a big old apple tree near the back steps of the house. At the sound, she looked around momentarily, shrugged, and went back to swinging. Max had been taking full advantage of the commotion, stealing birdseed from a feeder in the neighbor's backyard. When he heard the sound, he looked up and began barking.

"Quiet, Max!" Mother opened the back door and called. Max kept barking. With the next crack—a giant pop, almost as if something had exploded—we all turned around to look. The entire apple tree—including the limb upon which Kathy was swinging—was splitting. It seemed to be happening in slow motion. The tree was crashing down toward Kathy as Kathy was staring up at it. Still at the back door, my mother screamed; the rest of us yelled, but no one was able to move a muscle. No one except Max, that is.

The big dog bounded across the yard and grabbed the bottom of Kathy's parka in his jaws. He dragged her, protesting, out of the way—just

as the first branches crashed to the ground. In fact, he dragged her clear around to the front yard, leaving us all staring at the huge downed tree.

We ran to the front. Covered with snow, angry tears streaking her red face, Kathy was screaming at the oblivious Max. "What did you do that for, Max?" she sputtered.

Mother hugged her, and we hugged Max—until he pulled away to run back for more birdseed. Even an angel has to eat!

Routine Check-Up

*K*eith was preoccupied as he went out to check the plane. Sometimes it seemed a waste of time, he thought, that the pilots had to go back over all systems even though the mechanics had already checked everything. He turned on his flashlight. The tires looked fine. There were no flat spots. He glanced at the wear indicators for the brakes. No problems there. The hydraulic lines weren't leaking, and all the lights worked. Today as he mentally checked items off, he started wondering about his natural father. When he was younger, Keith's mother had mentioned that his dad had been an airplane mechanic. Although Keith had no plans to try to locate him, he'd always wondered if he might run into him sometime. After all, he often flew out of the airport where his father had been working at the time of Keith's birth.

"Wouldn't it be something," thought Keith, "if we met by chance sometime."

Confident that he'd rechecked everything, Keith climbed the steps back into the plane. He certainly hoped nothing would slow their departure tonight. The plane was headed into San Jose, and that airport had a landing curfew. If the plane didn't get there in time, they would have to land someplace else. Then there would be the hassle of having to get a hotel and rearranging his schedule for the morning. If that happened, he would probably never make it home in time for his daughter's first birthday party.

Maybe thinking of his own child was what had triggered thoughts of his natural father. He'd probably be retired by now, thought Keith, so there'd be no opportunity for a chance meeting.

Keith walked into the cabin and eased himself into the captain's chair. At 6′4″, conditions were a little cramped. Travelers had even less legroom; no wonder they were always complaining. Only 30 minutes until departure, and so far everything was moving on schedule. He radioed the tower for weather clearance.

The load master appeared in the doorway. He handed Keith the fuel slip. "Thirty-eight thousand pounds," he said, "and everything looks good on the ground."

They visited for a few minutes while Keith worked on his take-off data card. Using fuel weight, runway length, and air temperature, he calculated the safety of the planned take-off. "Looks like we're set," said Keith.

The load master waved good-bye and disappeared. Keith's copilot slipped into his seat, and, at Keith's urging, gave the initial welcome to the passengers. "On behalf of your captain and the flight crew, I'd like to welcome you aboard tonight's flight to San Jose. If that is not your planned destination, please exit the plane at this time." He paused to allow for the laughter that always followed those words.

"Flight 1054 has been cleared for take-off. In just a few minutes we will be closing the doors and pulling away from the jetway. As soon as we are airborne, the captain will give you more detailed flight information."

One of the flight attendants poked her head into the cockpit. "We've got all the passengers on board, and the luggage is on board. Shall we go ahead and close the doors?"

Keith gave the go-ahead and started on his before-start checklist. A commotion behind him broke his concentration. Someone was banging on the jetway door. One of those guys who's always late, thought Keith, and who's always lucky because people keep accommodating him. He wished he could teach the guy a lesson, but he knew what public relations would say about that. "Let him in," Keith called over his shoulder, "we'll hold."

Suddenly the load master burst into the cabin. "I couldn't get your attention, and you were already connected to the tower," he said as he wiped the sweat from his forehead. "Just as you were closing the doors this tall guy runs up to me. Says he's a retired mechanic, and that he just happened to be looking out the window when he sees a light reflect off something wet on the ground under number one engine. Tells me you should hold the flight because he thinks you've got a fuel leak."

Keith groaned. "Some guy just looks out the window and says we should stop the flight. I don't know. It's been less than 30 minutes since I checked. Think about what it'll cost the airline if we miss the landing curfew. Think about how irate the passengers are going to be. This will probably turn out to be nothing, but I guess we should at least take a look."

He grabbed his flashlight, and together they hurried down the stairs. Keith aimed the light at the ground under number one engine. There were spots on the pavement!

"I'll order a maintenance delay," said Keith.

"Somebody was sure watching over you," said the load master.

"I guess," said Keith. Could it have been his own father who had noticed the leak? Or was it his heavenly Father who had sent the warning? It didn't matter. Either way, someone had been looking out for him.

A man does not always choose what his guardian angel intends.
—Saint Thomas Aquinas

Navigation System

The young cow moose and her small, lop-eared calf, eating lush grass along the shore just below the dam, didn't even look up when I dumped out of my canoe. I was on a 100-mile canoe adventure, but this had turned more adventurous than I expected. The boulder I hit had been hidden, the split-second upset unexpected.

Fortunately, I thought inanely as the reality of the situation began to settle into my shocked mind, the wilderness ranger had our gear in his truck: tents, sleeping bags, clothing, food, towels, cooking equipment. He was taking it to the landing where I was heading. Or, I amended with an almost hysterical giggle as I came up for air, where my canoe was heading.

I had just time enough to look quickly around before I was sucked back under the water by the swift current. No one else from our group was in sight. They had apparently all made it to safety, upright and riding high.

Class III on the northern Maine river, the rapids were three miles of white water, eddies, swirls, snags, sweepers, strainers, and deep, deep pools of deceptive calm. The water was still chilly from the winter snows running off the higher mountains.

"Help!" I tried to call out, but a wave smacked me in the face. I choked and sputtered. As I passed an overhanging tree, I stretched to try and grab it, but the branch broke in my hand.

I panicked, choking and gasping, as I tumbled downriver, spinning head over heels, past rocks and dead branches lurking beneath the surface.

I was sure I was headed for certain death if I couldn't make it to shore before I came to the 40-foot waterfall ahead. Not only did scenes from my life pass before me, but a recent argument rose to the forefront. As I plunged pell-mell down the river, I had to laugh: I had won the argument but was, apparently, about to lose the point.

I had wanted to come on this wilderness hiking and canoeing trip when nobody else in the family had.

"Let's do something different," I had suggested to my family.

"Well, we can go to a different golf resort," my husband helpfully (and hopefully) offered.

"Yeah, Mom, or a new theme park. One with lots of new rides," said the children, jumping up and down in their excitement.

That wasn't what I had in mind at all, but here I was, where I had said I wanted to be, doing something different.

Caught for a moment in a pool of calm, I hoped that help might be close. I treaded water, my boots and heavy clothing trying to drag me below the surface.

Our guide had taken his canoe first to be on hand to help the group members make it to shore at the landing. The landing was no more than a piece of shore jutting out into the river. Once it had anchored half a bridge, the guide told us around last night's campfire, but the fast-running river, swollen and angry with ice, had clipped it like a linebacker in a football game, bringing the bridge crashing down. We were told to avoid going past the landing because there were chunks of concrete with metal re-bar still attached, waiting to snag unwary canoeists.

When you're worried about someone you care for, cast your thoughts, prayers, and wishes to their angel. Love them from a distance, then move on knowing they are in good hands.

Surely our guide or someone from the group who'd arrived safely would wonder where I was and come back to look for me.

I had a sudden image of my empty canoe appearing in the center of the waiting group. My children and husband would be wild with worry.

And, no matter how worried he might be, my husband wouldn't be able to resist thinking "I told you so!" I would allow and even forgive him a big "I TOLD YOU SO!" if only I could survive my own folly.

I cried silently, the sound of the racing water drowning out my sobs. "I love you," I shouted across the watery gap. I thought of my husband trying to raise the children without me. He was an excellent father but too busy to give them all the time and attention they needed. I longed to feel his skin beneath my hands, hands that were getting scraped against the gravel river bottom each time the current shoved me under. Who would make his coffee every morning and put love notes in his brown-bag lunches?

I pushed my thoughts to my children, who I might never see again. I couldn't bear to think of them motherless.

They had ridden the rapids with the ranger because this was such a rough patch of white water. Spring had been harsh, and the water was especially high, making currents faster and rocks, which were usually visible, booby traps you couldn't see until too late.

I felt sobs trying to escape, only to be choked off by the water I was swallowing. My shoulder grazed a sharp rock, and I nearly became wedged between two flat stones; only the force of the water pulled me forward, like a cork from a bottle. I was drowning, the serenity of oxygen deprivation lulling me into giving up. All advice and canoeing tips our guide had given us were being shaken from me.

Suddenly I heard a voice calling to me, "Float feet first, float feet first." A hand on my shoulder stopped my pell-mell somersaulting.

Yes! I thought, that was what I was supposed to do if I tipped over in the rapids.

Sticking my boots out in front of me, I began to float feet first. I remembered that this rule was so your head was protected. Gradually, I got my bearings and tried to steer myself toward the open channel of water in the center of the river. Thoughts of the waterfall loomed in my mind, but I was strangely calm. I was not alone. The guide who'd coached me about floating feet first would help me make it to safety.

The water grew more shallow and warmer, the rocks smaller. I managed to swim to a large, flat-topped rock where I rested for a few minutes. I had no choice but to keep going. Shore was sheer cliffs on both sides through this part of the rapids. I eased myself back into the current and, floating feet first, bobbed on down the river, led to move this way or that way by the guide's voice.

I heard the cheering even before I saw the group. I rounded a final bend and there they were, waiting at the landing, applauding and shouting as I came into view. Our guide, wearing the traditional black-and-red–checkered shirt, stood knee-deep in the water holding my canoe by its rope.

I more or less washed ashore, where I clung to my husband and cried over the children, much to their disgust.

Wrapped in a blanket and drinking hot coffee, I thanked the guide for his advice. "I would have drowned if you hadn't been there."

He stared at me. "But I wasn't there…I thought you would be OK." He hadn't even seen me capsize—it'd happened around the bend at a blind spot, he explained. He'd only known I was in trouble when my canoe floated toward him.

I felt again that steadying hand on my shoulder and heard that calming, firm voice that had interrupted my panic. "Float feet first, float feet first."

When we were ready to launch canoes from the far side of the landing and continue on, I used my paddle to hold me steady in the shallows as I turned and faced the boulder-strewn obstacle course behind me. I wished I could thank my guide properly, for I had learned a life lesson about not being alone. Being dunked in the rapids had been worth it, I wanted to tell him. But not all guides wear black-and-red–checkered shirts and stand on shore; some wade in deep waters and stay mostly out of sight.

Day of Reckoning

We all face a day of reckoning. We find ourselves there when we have run as far as we can, for as long as we can.

I had just finished writing my suicide note. I left it for my three daughters on the front seat of my car. I wanted them to understand, from my own words, what had driven me to this moment.

It was 1992: I'll always remember it as the worst year of my life. My one blessing had been a new baby girl, but even that happiness had come at great cost, since we discovered during the pregnancy that something was seriously wrong with my heart. I had spent much of the pregnancy in the cardiac care unit of the local hospital. Right after my baby was born, I was moved to another hospital in another city for intensive care and diagnostics. Because my heart was so weak, the doctors would not let me hold my baby girl for a month and a half. It was a horribly lonely and difficult time for me.

Then, when I finally returned home, weak in body and spirit, I sensed that all was not well there, either. I learned that my husband had not brought our new baby home during my long stay in the hospital but had paid professional sitters to keep and care for her. And soon I heard rumors about my husband and another woman. But that couldn't be true, could it? The "other woman" was my best friend, someone I'd shared so much laughter, love, and sorrow with over the years. So I ignored the talk and tried not to notice the small signs that sometimes nagged at me. We maintained an uneasy peace for six months; my heart, after all, was still too weak for such a shock. But then one night, with our baby yet an infant and my health still fragile, my husband did not come home. My best friend, as it turned out, was with him.

I had been married to this man for 16 years! We had three lovely daughters, a comfortable home, and a business we had built ourselves, together. Suddenly, I was alone, in my thirties, with a new baby and two teenage girls, a heart that was giving out, and a marriage that was over. All the security I'd known had been shattered.

I felt so alone, so rejected by the husband I still loved. Still loved! How could I? He'd abandoned me and, together with my best friend, had betrayed me. I begged God to take the love from my heart, but my prayers seemed to be in vain. I cried out to God: *Why have you turned your back on me?* I was physically and emotionally drained.

Was I searching for God's attention when I parked my car at 2 A.M. that Sunday morning? Maybe I was afraid he didn't love me, or maybe I was afraid he just might.

I knew there would be no traffic on the bridge leading out of town in the middle of night. No one would notice that I had slipped quietly away. I would jump into the river and let God do with me whatever he saw fit. As I climbed to the highest point on the bridge, I could feel the tears spilling down my cheeks and the breeze of the cool night air.

At the precise moment I stood up to leap, a hand touched mine and held it tight. I turned my head and saw a man, a stranger.

He said, "Lady, I don't know what's happening here, but as I drove over this bridge, something or someone said as plain as day: *Turn around, now, and go back!* I didn't want to go back! But all of a sudden my wheel started turning in my hand, and I couldn't make it stop. Then, as I was heading back over the bridge, I saw you. It must have been an angel who turned that wheel—it certainly wasn't me. So don't jump. *Please* don't jump. God sent me to hold your hand."

As he spoke, a sense of peace settled over me. I knew I was supposed to step back off that bridge. I let the man help me down. When I looked up, police cars were all around us.

Over the next few weeks, as I began to recover, I felt ashamed that I had almost taken my life just because another human being had let me down. I now saw clearly that there was someone who had been there all along, someone who cared for me and promised to stay with me always.

But my difficulties were not over yet: I had a divorce to get through, I would have to stay on heart medication for the rest of my life, and I was a single mother with two teenagers and a baby. But in spite of all this, the peace I'd felt that night on the bridge—when a stranger stood next to me, holding my hand and talking of God's love—stayed with me. I had felt a new sense of security, a different, deeper security that sprang from a

renewed trust in God, from a certainty that, somehow, our lives would be all right.

After that, the pieces of my life started to fit into place. I began to gain insights into what had gone wrong. I was able to let go, to start over emotionally, to stop dwelling on the past. And, with the Lord's help, I was able to learn forgiveness. That was perhaps the hardest task of all, but I eventually truly forgave both my husband and my friend, and it's a wonderful feeling to have that resentment taken away. There is no end to what the Lord has done for me; every day I see him at work in the lives of my three wonderful daughters.

I've tried many times to find out something, anything, about the man who helped me that night on the bridge. I often think about him; I wish I could thank him for saving my life. But no one remembers him. The police don't recall talking with him, nor was he mentioned in any police reports. He never told me his name, and I can't remember much about what he looked like. I think he had brown hair and brown eyes, but I'm not even sure about that. He was just an average man, guided by God's angels to help an average woman. God reached out to touch two ordinary hearts on a bridge that night, and both of us learned of God's extraordinary love.

Cover Me

Women in their 40s just don't get record deals. That's what Felicia Cole's best friend, Marly, had told her. As Felicia stood at her mailbox that morning holding another rejection note and returned demo tape, she sighed with resignation. Maybe Marly was right. Maybe becoming a singer/songwriter was just a pipe dream, a possibility for someone far younger and more resilient than Felicia.

Felicia went into the small duplex she owned and closed the door behind her. She stared at the tape, tempted to toss it into the trash, along with her dreams. Instead, she put it in the drawer of her hall desk and decided to take a long, brisk walk to burn off her frustration. She put on her sweats, grabbed her keys, and headed outside.

It was a beautiful day, and, before she knew it, Felicia had logged three miles. She slowed down once to let two fire engines pass, curious as to where they were heading. As she rounded the bend heading back home, she could see smoke rising into the sky. Whatever was burning was close.

Back on her street, Felicia's heart stopped cold. The smoke was pouring out of her neighbor's home, which was attached to hers. She ran full tilt, through the fire trucks and the firefighters milling around. Ignoring their warnings, she flew past them to her front door, unlocking it and racing inside. One firefighter chased after her, urging her to get out, and Felicia could see why. The flames had already passed through the common wall and now her home was on fire.

She screamed above the noise of falling beams and hissing smoke that she had to find her cat, Macy. The firefighter followed Felicia into a back room, yelling for her to come with him, but Felicia was on the floor reaching under the bed, where Macy was hiding. As Felicia reached to grab Macy, she heard a groaning noise. Just two feet behind her the ceiling fell

in, showering pieces of rubble and wood that now stood between her and the firefighter who scrambled to get her free.

As the flames made their way into the hall just outside the back bedroom, Felicia understood the stupidity of her move. She was trapped. But at least Macy had jumped out of her arms and had run to safety out the open window in the adjacent bathroom. The firefighter, who told her his name was Bill, shouted at her to stay still, that he was coming to get her. He asked her name, and talked to her in a comforting tone, telling her it would be all right.

But Felicia wasn't so sure it would be all right. Smoke filled the room and her lungs, and she fought to stay low to the ground. She began coughing violently, feeling weaker with each passing breath. Bill's voice seemed to be getting farther and farther away. But she could feel him gently pick her up and carry her in strong, capable arms through the fire and smoke. Then everything turned to blackness.

When she next opened her eyes, Felicia was in an ambulance on the way to the hospital. She kept asking about the firefighter who rescued her, but the paramedic kept working and looking at her quizzically. He assured her that all the firefighters were fine.

She spent the next two days in the hospital. When she was released to her mother's care, the first thing Felicia did, even before calling the insurance company, was to pick up a notepad and pen and write the words to what would become a song called "Cover Me."

> *Cover me, in times of trouble,*
> *Cover me, in times of despair.*
> *In your heart I can always find comfort.*
> *In your arms I have nothing to fear.*

One month later, Felicia stood at the mailbox of the apartment she was renting until her home was rebuilt. This time, the letter was not a rejection; it was an invitation to go to Los Angeles to talk with a major record company about a possible recording deal. They had loved her song "Cover Me" and thought it had hit potential. Felicia rushed inside to call the name and number on the letter to confirm, but she then decided to do something else first.

At the local fire station, just three blocks away, she rang the bell. A young man answered. Felicia asked if she could speak to Bill. The young man gave her a funny look, answering that there was no Bill there. Felicia insisted, telling him she was the one Bill rescued from the burning duplex. The young man just shook his head, then motioned for her to come inside.

Felicia waited in the TV room. An older man walked in and introduced himself. He told Felicia that he had been one of the firefighters on

duty the day of the fire, and he reiterated that there was no firefighter named Bill, or William for that matter, on the roster. He looked surprised when Felicia asked who, then, had carried her out of the building. He told Felicia that no one had carried her out, that she had crawled through the rubble and fire on her own, and that he and everyone present had thought it miraculous that she had made it out alive.

But there had been no firefighter named Bill.

Felicia was confused, but she thanked the man and turned to walk back home. They had to be wrong, she thought, for she had seen his caring eyes and heard his comforting voice. She had felt the strength of his arms as he carried her over pieces of burning wood and through the suffocating black smoke.

For the rest of that day Felicia wondered what indeed had happened to her. But in her heart she believed that an angel named Bill had saved her life.

Her angel had truly covered her in her time of trouble.

Angels are all around us, as far as the heart can see.

A Welcome Interruption

Many of us like to believe that we have guardian angels watching out for us. On one January day a few years ago, my cousin Beau turned out to be an angel in disguise.

Arriving home from work at 5:00, I put a cold weather staple, a pot of beef stew, on top of the stove to heat. My sister, Mil, with whom I shared a house, was detained at the bank and wouldn't be home until 6:30. Tired from a pressured day of proofreading and editing manuscripts in the graphic arts firm where I worked, I decided to lie down on the living room sofa. I quickly fell asleep.

The doorbell rang. I resented the interruption, so I decided to ignore it. Then Beau's pleasant face appeared in the door's glass top, so, of course, I had to get up. I was groggy and wished he hadn't awakened me, though I always enjoyed visiting with him.

I noticed with surprise that he was carrying his toolbox. Fortunately for me and Mil (because of our limited finances), Beau was a household Mr. Fix-it. I suddenly recalled that he had promised to reinforce our worn kitchen cabinets on Wednesday—they were about to fall off the wall. But this was Tuesday.

As I let him in, I couldn't help remarking, "We got our dates mixed, Beau. I was expecting you tomorrow. But that's all right. If you'd rather do the work this afternoon. . . ."

Puzzled, he hesitated on the threshold.

"You're right, Wyn!" he said, slapping his thigh. "I remember now, I *did* say Wednesday. Gosh, I'm sorry. Go back to your nap—I'll drop by tomorrow."

I searched for the correct words. It would never do to hurt his feelings. However, I was longing to rest. "Perhaps that would be better," I began. "That is, if you'd rather. I've had an exhausting day."

Looking intently behind me, Beau did not answer. He just sniffed and then shouted: "What's that smell? Gas!"

He raced past me, through the living room and into the kitchen. Bewildered, and now conscious of a sweet, sickish odor, I dropped to the sofa.

"I've found the trouble," he called excitedly. "The stove's turned on under the stew, but the burner's not lit. I'll shut off the range and open some windows and doors to let the gas escape. In a few minutes it would have flooded the place. But fresh air will make short work of it."

Relieved and satisfied, he rejoined me in the living room.

"Don't worry, the danger's over," he said. "You're lucky, Wyn. That leak could have knocked you to kingdom come if you had kept on sleeping."

The fresh air was an invigorating tonic. I sat up straight and smiled at him.

"I think you saved my life, Beau. I can never thank you enough."

"Don't thank me," he grinned. "Thank the guy upstairs, who tipped me off," he said as he pointed to heaven.

144

Angel With Four Paws

The night had turned cold when Martha finally ended her shift at the restaurant. She stepped outside to head home. It had been a very busy night, with truckers coming in nonstop from the highway throughout the night, and Martha had worked two hours overtime to make sure everyone got what they needed. As dog-tired and aching as her feet were, she could certainly use the extra money.

She crossed the street and headed toward the tiny parking lot where she usually parked her car, but the lot was full of trucks and she couldn't spot her small Honda anywhere. Martha stood there for a moment, certain that the hectic shift had gotten to her brain, wondering where on earth she had parked her car. Then she remembered the lot had been full when she got there. She had parked at Lew's Deli, on the street behind the diner. She ran across the street, scolding herself for being so forgetful. She was working way too hard these days; sometimes her brain just couldn't keep up with all she had to remember.

She headed down the alley to the next street south, certain her vehicle would be right in front of Lew's, which was now closed. It wasn't there. Martha felt a tiny ball of panic begin to bounce in the pit of her stomach. She took a deep breath, not wanting the panic to get any bigger. Her car had to be here somewhere, unless, and she hated even giving the thought credence, it had been stolen. Just then she heard a rustling behind her. Turning, she saw a dark shadow in the alley. Panic bore down on her like

a freight train as she realized she was within attack distance of a huge, ominous-looking black dog.

The beast had to be almost as big as her, and she wasn't short. Or maybe it was just the eerie way the street lamp cast a glow on the animal, which appeared to be some kind of mutt, albeit a big and threatening one. The dog moved a step toward Martha, its fierce yellow eyes trained on her. Martha felt her throat catch as she tried to scream, to cry out for help.

146

Nothing came out but a soft whimper. She forced her feet to move and took a wobbly step backward. The dog responded, taking another step forward, and Martha realized that she only had two choices: Stay and be attacked, or run and be attacked.

Choosing the latter, Martha held her breath and ran from the dog. She rushed down another alley leading back to the diner. She didn't dare look back, but she heard the thud of the dog's heavy paws following her. She dodged between cars and trucks in the side lot, trying desperately to find her car, and she slammed right up against the cab of a pickup. It took the wind out of her for a second, long enough for her to see the dog coming out of the shadows toward her. She turned, frozen with fear, to face the dog, certain she was about to be attacked. She tried again to scream, to get a word out of her tight throat, but she could barely croak a whisper. "Why won't you leave me alone?" she hissed at the dog, but the animal stared at her with golden slits of eyes.

Voices off to the side of the lot caught Martha's attention. Gasping for strength, she forced her body in motion, figuring if the dog attacked her now, at least she would have some help. As she followed the voices, she found her own voice again and was about to scream for help when she noticed the source of the voices. She had found her car, parked where she left it in a small alley next to the diner. But she also found two large and very hostile-looking young men in her car, trying to hot-wire it.

As she turned to run before they could see or hear her, the two men looked up. Sensing the threat, they got out of the car and came menacingly toward her. One of them brandished a long knife, and Martha froze

as the other man put his hand in his pocket and motioned as if he had a gun. She was about to concede her Honda to them, beg them to take it if they would just let her go, when she heard a fierce growl behind her. In a flash of dark fury, the dog that had been following her lunged past her, landing squarely on the two men, knocking them over and attacking them. Martha screamed full force over and over again. Within a minute, several truckers who had just left the diner came to her rescue.

The truckers pinned down the two bloodied and defeated car thieves as Martha ran to the diner to call the police, stopping only to look back at the wonderful dog that had clearly been following her to protect her. But the dog was nowhere in sight.

Ten minutes later the police arrived, questioning Martha and the truckers. Martha told them about the dog, and when the officer did a quick check of the two suspects, the bite marks were evident. The dog had vanished, and now the suspects would have to deal with the possibility of rabies.

But Martha knew, as she got into her Honda to head home, that her guardian angel wasn't rabid. As she pulled out onto the main road something made her glance over to the alley opposite of where the police were finishing their work. There, in the shadows, she could see two bright yellow eyes staring at her. Martha stopped her car, rolled down her window, and whispered "Thank you." As she drove away, she knew she would see that dog again, perhaps on another cold night when she had worked an extra-long shift and her feet were tired and aching.

Night-light

*I*t had been a mistake to come to the cabin. It was too soon. The six months since Dorothy's death weren't nearly enough to blur Marc's memories of their life together. But it was Memorial Day weekend and he could think of no place he'd rather be.

Just driving down the dirt road sent him bouncing back in time. They'd bounced along it together years ago hoping to hasten the baby's arrival. How they'd laughed when Steven was born that very night.

The pine tree by the bend in the road brought tears to his eyes. He shook his head to make them go away. He remembered he'd shaken his head at their naïveté when, years ago, they'd brought up their potted Christmas tree to plant beside their mountain retreat. Neither of them had realized it would be impossible to dig in the frozen January ground. They'd brought the tree back up the next spring. It had been smaller than little Sarah then. Now it towered above his head. He'd wanted Dorothy to see it last Christmas, but she'd been too weak. The cancer too advanced.

Where had the time gone? Somehow their 33 years of marriage seemed shorter than their last six months together. He could see the flannel nightgown Dorothy had been wearing that last morning of her life more clearly than the beautiful tulle dress she'd worn on their wedding day. The memory of the night-light he kept on so she wouldn't be frightened when she woke in pain eclipsed his memory of the lighthouse night-light they'd picked out for the kids when they had vacationed in Cape Cod. The names of the hospice volunteers came to his mind more quickly than the names of their lifelong friends.

Dorothy's death had been a blessing. That's what everyone had said. He opened the cabin door. The smell of the potpourri she'd made last summer overwhelmed him. She'd dried the flowers just days before the doctor gave them the dire prognosis. Inoperable, incurable, inescapable.

She'd been so brave... only begging for mercy and medication at the very end when the pain was no longer bearable. It wasn't until her death that he'd ever thought, even for a moment, that her dying might be preferable to her living.

Marc dropped onto the couch in front of the wood-burning stove. They'd sat in front of it together for the last time when they'd come up in early September to see the aspens. The bright green leaves of summer had already begun to change to the color of copper pennies. Even then he realized Dorothy was changing too, moving away from her earthly life.

He laid a fire. If he could force himself to stay the weekend he'd need it for warmth. Nights were always cold in the Rockies. Marc could even remember one Memorial Day weekend when it had snowed. He and Dorothy and the kids had roasted marshmallows and played a marathon game of Monopoly. They'd snuggled together that night beneath several layers of blankets.

"Oh, God," Marc thought, "why didn't you take me too?" Suddenly he knew he had to get out of the cabin. He grabbed the old denim jacket that hung on the door and plunged out into the evening. He headed down the river to Horizon Point, a high steep peek with a panoramic view.

Marc started his upward climb. Almost unconsciously he began making a plan. He could "accidentally" fall from the top. Every summer one or two people were killed climbing in the Rockies. He'd left no note and never mentioned suicide so no one would be the wiser. By the time he approached the tree line, rain splatted on the rocks beside him. So much the better, he thought. People would think he'd slipped.

The temperature was dropping rapidly, and the rain was mixing with snow. What a release death would be. He wouldn't have to endure the loneliness any longer. As he trudged upward, he remembered the times he'd led the family on this very same hike. "Our fearless leader," Dorothy had teased.

That was how Dorothy had thought of him. Her last words had been "Love the kids for both of us." Marc was suddenly ashamed. How could he ever have thought of ignoring Dorothy's dying wish. He'd been selfish to think only of himself. Steven and Sarah had lost their mother. They needed him. Aware of the cold for the first time, Marc buttoned his jacket. It had been stupid to go climbing at this time of year without warmer clothing.

Snow swirled around him. The path disappeared. Disoriented, he paused to think. He had to get back to the cabin somehow. He'd freeze if he stayed on the mountain. He knew he needed to head down, but where

was down? If he went the wrong way, he'd probably fall from the cliff that rose above the river. The choice of living or dying no longer seemed his to make.

He inched his way over the rocks, hoping he was still on the trail. Then, through the snow and the late afternoon darkness, he thought he saw a light. It couldn't be from the cabin. He hadn't turned one on. Still, he decided he'd head for it.

Cautiously he descended until he reached the shelter of the trees. He saw that he was on the trail. As he followed it back to the cabin, he saw that the light that had guided him through the darkness was coming from his car.

On closer inspection, he discovered that his seat belt had caught in the door, preventing it from closing completely and so keeping the dome light on. He thought of the night-light he'd always left on for Dorothy. Maybe God turned on night-lights, too.

Angel in My Pocket

I lay unclaimed on the sandy beach, waterlogged and half-drowned. I was only seven years old, and as far as the strangers who crowded around me were concerned, I was completely alone.

Everyone seemed to be staring at me. Someone was shouting questions: "What is your name, little girl?" and "Where do you live?" But my lungs were filled with the seawater I had swallowed, and I could not speak.

I am 78 years old now, but I can still picture the incident as clearly as if it had happened yesterday. The place was Westcliffe-on-Sea, a popular seaside resort in England. We were there on holiday. My normally jocular father was attempting to recuperate from a serious bout of rheumatic fever, and the laughter had temporarily gone out of our lives.

Mother was a small, fragile woman, trying desperately to cope with three rambunctious children and nurse my sick father back to health at the same time. On the morning in question, my boisterous brother had been invited to play with some friends he'd made nearby. Then, when some older girls we'd met asked if they could take me down to the beach to play, my mother readily agreed. She assured them that she'd be down soon with my little sister.

But once we were on the beach, the other girls forgot about me and ran away. I was alone. While waiting for my mother, I decided to paddle in the water. Suddenly a huge wave carried me along and dragged me under.

The presence of an angel is like a snowflake lightly touching you with its special gift, then evaporating into your warmth as you hurry on your way.

I distinctly recall coming up three times, and then the water was over my head. I was frightened, but a lovely lady, with long, blonde hair and wearing a silver swimsuit, cradled me in her arms and laid me gently on the beach. Then she disappeared, but I knew she was "the angel in my pocket."

Mother was always telling us about the angels on earth helping people in distress. I used to say I kept an angel in my pocket, because when something bad nearly happened my angel would always protect me. This time proved I was right.

A gentleman from the crowd knelt beside me and turned me over. I remember a lot of water pouring from my mouth. Just as an ambulance arrived to take me to the hospital, my mother appeared with my little sister. She had come down to find me and, seeing a crowd, went to see what was happening. When she saw me and the ambulance nearby, she fainted.

My mother said she would never have let me paddle along the water's edge if she had known how rough the sea was. Apparently, the waters were so abnormally wild that day that three good swimmers had drowned. The girls who were to have watched me were nowhere to be seen.

Eventually, when things were back to normal, my parents tried to find out who had saved my life. Such a heroic gesture deserved to be rewarded. But I for one knew no one would ever come forward, because the angel in my pocket had flown away to help someone else in need.

From Darkness Into Light

Newspaper headlines in South Florida for Thursday, December 22, 1988, carried a chilling account of a family abducted and held for ransom by three men armed with automatic weapons. The *Sun-Sentinel* in Fort Lauderdale story ran: "$250,000 Kidnaping Ransom Paid, Thrift Chief's Family Freed From Car's Trunk." *The Miami Herald* said: "3 Hold Bank Chief and Family, Flee With Nearly $250,000."

Until that day, I hadn't given much thought to God and angels, I'm sorry to say. I was a workaholic mom, recently remarried, and preoccupied with climbing the corporate ladder, not the one to heaven. For the first nine years of my life, God had been a security guard of sorts—someone I called upon only in times of need. I knew he was there, but I never really paid much attention to him. Today, God is...well, everything in my life. And I give thanks a thousand times a day. I wouldn't be here to tell you my story if it weren't for his guardian angels who heard my desperate cry.

That Tuesday in 1988, my new husband and I attended a routine dinner meeting with some clients. About 7:00 P.M., I called home to see if everything was all right and to tell my housekeeper we'd be home around 10:00. But when I spoke with her, she had a strange tone in her voice that made me uneasy, even though she said everything was fine. During dinner, I kept looking at my watch. I could feel it—something just didn't sit right. The knot in my stomach got tighter as we approached the house. As I

opened the door, I saw three men standing in our living room with guns pointed at us.

I turned and ran down the driveway, screaming. A man wearing a wig and carrying an automatic weapon came after me and pushed me down. "Shut up!" he ordered. "I won't hurt you, but you have to be quiet." He dragged me back inside. My husband was lying on the floor with his arms wrenched behind his back.

"Relax. We're not going to hurt you. We're just here to rob the bank," shouted one of the men.

"Where's my daughter?" I said, shaking and crying.

"Where's your purse?" he demanded.

After he took our cash, watches, and jewelry, again I begged, "Please, I have to go see my daughter." The lead man escorted me upstairs. My daughter was safe, thank God, but my housekeeper looked horrified. I hugged them both in the dimly lit bedroom and tried to muffle my sobs. The men ordered my husband upstairs, also.

"In the morning, you will fill this duffel bag with cash," one of the men said, tossing it on the bed.

They called themselves "One," "Two," and "Three," and they took turns standing guard throughout the night. We could hear the others snoring. They all wore wigs, sunglasses, and ridiculous-looking caps. Morning seemed forever away. I whispered to my daughter, "Let's go to sleep," and we huddled under the covers. My husband and our housekeeper were lying on the floor. I never closed my eyes. My mind was empty, nearly numb with fear.

It was still dark out at 5:30 A.M. when we were awakened and ordered outside.

"Now, you two, into the trunk," ordered One, waving and pointing at my daughter and me with his gun.

"Oh, no, please don't put us in the trunk," I pleaded.

"Mommy, what are we doing?" my daughter asked in desperation.

"We're going to play hide-and-seek," I said nervously.

We curled up in the fetal position, and, as the car began to move, I focused on the red glow of the taillights and the monotonous bumping of the tires. The only thing keeping me from going crazy was my young daughter. We held each other tightly, and instinctively I started singing "Baa, Baa, Black Sheep," "The Itsy Bitsy Spider"...anything I could think of to help pretend this wasn't happening.

After being driven for what seemed like hours, the car stopped, doors slammed, and we heard muffled voices that got fainter and fainter. I was certain they had left us in the Everglades to die. The heat of the day was in full force, and the trunk felt like a sauna. We were breathing the same air over and over again. I kept saying to myself: *My God, I don't know if we can survive, I don't know if we can survive.* My chant became almost rhythmic as I rocked back and forth while I was holding my daughter cradled against me.

By now we were hungry, and we were hot and cramped. I didn't want us to fall asleep for fear we'd breathe carbon dioxide and never wake up. At some point, I gave up. "Let's close our eyes and take a nap," I whispered gently.

When I closed my eyes, I began to pray. And even though I don't remember ever memorizing Psalm 23, the words came clearly to my mind: *The Lord is my shepherd, I shall not want. . . .*

When I finished the entire psalm, I told God that if it was my time to die, he could take me. I surrendered. But my daughter didn't deserve this. At that moment, I left my body through a tunnel of light. My eyes were closed, yet I could see an incredible energy enveloping me. I was surrounded by gossamer beings of light, and though I could not see them, their voices sounded in my mind. "Susie," they said, "there is nothing to be afraid of. You are protected by God and your angels." It gave me such a peaceful feeling, a feeling of pure love.

"Where am I?" I asked.

"It doesn't matter," they answered. "You are with God, and it's not your time. You are not going to die."

I felt like I was hovering, and I turned and could still see the car below, when they added, "You have much yet to do and to accomplish, and we are here with you."

In a flash, I was back in the trunk with a thud that frightened my daughter, and she started to cry.

Just then, I looked up and saw a quarter-size hole in the trunk that I had not seen before. I told my daughter, "God is with us and the angels

are with us." She clearly didn't understand what I was talking about, but I finally felt hope that we might survive.

Soon we were bathed in light. I could see the clear blue sky and some telephone wires, so I knew we were in town and not in the Everglades. I wanted to make sure I wasn't going crazy, so I asked my daughter, "Can you see the hole and the sky and feel the fresh air?" "Yes, Mommy," she said, "where did it come from?"

"It's from God and the angels he sent to protect us," I said, kissing her hair and rocking back and forth. I knew then that we would be safe because someone or something heavenly had intervened.

A short while later, we were rescued by a group of police officers, with my husband and some bank officials greeting us with relief and thankfulness. It was a moment of rebirth, literally.

When some of the confusion surrounding the scene settled, I turned to look at the trunk that had nearly become our coffin. I saw tiny dents, but I couldn't find the quarter-size opening. It was no longer there.

Had we only imagined it? Or had we been saved by the hand of God?

I don't have any proof, of course. But what I've learned over the last ten years is that when science and logic and reality have no good explanation for something, that's when faith takes over.

My life is different now. I am different. My world has been inextricably altered, although nothing's changed except the way I look at it. I would not wish the experience that transformed my existence on anyone. Yet, for me, it has been a gift, a blessing, and I wouldn't change it.

If it took this to bring the awakening of God into my heart, then it was worth it. I don't want to mislead you— it wasn't a magical, overnight transformation. It took time. I struggled with the emotional aftermath of post-traumatic stress disorder and fought the fear, paranoia, and depression that threatened to consume me. I didn't immediately recognize the gift I'd been given, nor did I understand why I'd been given it. Finding answers to those questions took me on a long and arduous journey. But the answers took many forms and brought me to where I am today.

About the only thing I would change if it were up to me would be those headlines in the papers. They should have read: "God Sends Angels From Heaven to Rescue Kidnap Victims," or maybe, "Heavenly Intervention Saves Mother and Child." But then, those kinds of headlines belong on supermarket tabloids. Who believes those kinds of stories anyway, right?

Rock-a-bye Baby

I was pumping as high as I dared in the white wicker swing on our sprawling front porch that sultry Southern summer afternoon. The air was fragrant with frothy pink mimosa blossoms, new-mown grass, and pavements freshly washed by the street sweeper. Steam rose from the puddles that dusty birds dipped and splashed in.

I was serving as lookout for the cousins' arrival.

They were driving all the way from New Mexico to a family reunion this evening here at our house in the East Tennessee hills.

There had been a lot of "tsk-tsking" and head shaking from my grandmother, my mother, and my aunts when the southwestern relatives had announced they would be driving to the reunion. There was another baby on the way for their family. Number five.

I was too young to understand that cross-country trips and babies on the way were not necessarily the best traveling companions. All I knew was that it sounded like an adventure to me. I hadn't been beyond the city limits in my whole eight years of life.

The time of arrival came and went.

No one, though, really thought much about it. My family was known for showing up with seconds to spare for weddings, funerals, school, church. The preacher had even gotten to where he checked to see if we were seated before he started in. I figured he'd gotten tired of being upstaged as we traipsed in trying to be quiet.

Soon, though, the entire family joined me on the front porch, chasing stray breezes.

All the cooking was done right down to having the lemons squeezed, the mint ready to toss into it. The fried chicken and roast beef were being

kept warm, and the biscuits were just waiting to be mixed up and popped in the oven. Picnic hampers carried from cars by shirt-sleeved uncles sat ready to be opened and shared. My mouth watered.

The telephone rang.

Mama answered it with a breathless question in her voice. "Hello?"

After a pause that was longer than necessary to tell us they would be just a little late, Mama said, "Thank God."

"There's been an accident," she turned to say, covering the receiver with her hand.

"No one is hurt. They are taking tests to make sure the baby is OK," she told the assembled kith and kin.

How could you test a baby that wasn't born yet? I didn't understand. What I did comprehend, however, was that something amazing had happened and it was going to make supper a little bit late but worth the wait.

Later that afternoon, in my bath towel/Superman cape, I was standing on the porch railing when the cousins' car finally turned the corner.

I let out a hoop 'n' a holler, and everyone came running just as the cousins pulled up in a rented car. I could tell it was rented because there was no dent in the passenger side and no broken headlights, no mangled tires. That was all the detail Mama had been able to get from my uncle.

The four children, the cousins I'd been waiting for, clambered from the car and ran into our grandmother's waiting arms. My Aunt Callie was the last one to step from the car, escorted from the passenger side on the arm of my uncle who bent to help her. And then, to my utter astonishment, he turned back and gently lifted a black-and-white dog from the front seat. Its leg was bandaged, and the dog hobbled a bit when Uncle Willie set it down on the grass.

It looked up questioningly at my aunt. "Come on," she said to the dog, stooping awkwardly to stroke its back. "I want you to meet your family." She turned to us. "This little fella has a story to tell," she said softly.

"Let's eat first," Mama said, worrying about the chicken and roast beef in the oven, the ice melting in the lemonade.

Aunt Callie smiled. "The story will keep," she said, looking up at Uncle Willie. He bent down and carefully picked up the dog and carried him to the front porch to settle him with the first slice of roast beef—and he served it on a real dinner plate, much to Mama's displeasure. But Mama didn't say anything, just clamped her mouth shut like she does sometimes. Oh, boy, did she have to eat crow later on that one!

The rest of the evening passed in a blur of ". . . pass the chicken, cole slaw, potato salad, butter-dripping biscuits with homemade strawberry jam." After which we cut into the watermelon and followed it with the traditional seed-spitting contest. I came in second.

We didn't get around to hearing the rest of the story about the dog until after supper, when everyone was sitting on the porch taking turns cranking the ice-cream freezers. The dog lay, one eye open, at my aunt's feet. The squeak of the twin rocking chairs where my grandparents sat was accompanied by the swishing of lawn sprinklers; lightning bugs flickered on the distant hillside.

"There we were, making good time even with a steady hard rain and all the potty stops," my Aunt Callie said, beginning the tale with an affec-

tionate smile at her two youngest children, now sleeping soundly on the old chaise lounge.

"And then all of a sudden she shouted, 'STOP!'" said Uncle Willie, picking up the story.

"A black-and-white dog," he continued, "was standing smack dab in the middle of the road not two car lengths away."

As one, we all stared at the dog, finally sleeping soundly, apparently oblivious to our interest.

Uncle Willie, according to the story as it unfolded, pulled the station wagon off the highway and, at Aunt Callie's insistence, went back to see if the dog was OK. It followed him back to the car, jumped in, and settled on Callie's lap.

"Licking my hand, as if to say 'Thanks,' it turned in a circle and went to sleep right there in my lap!" Aunt Callie said.

Speechless, she and Uncle Willie had looked at one another. But they were already late to our house and the reunion and didn't have time to find an animal shelter, they explained.

"We neither one had the heart to leave the dog on the highway," volunteered Uncle Willie, taking a long pull on a glass of mint-sprigged lemonade.

Especially, they laughed, when the children pointed out the dog apparently didn't appear to have enough sense to get in out of the rain!

"The baby seemed to like the dog sitting so close," Aunt Callie said, rubbing her stomach now. "This little baby stretched out a tiny foot right

at the dog lying next to it until I knew it could feel it! That's when I told Willie that it looked to me like we were going to have a new baby and a pet!"

They were still laughing about that when a truck ran a stop sign and rammed into their station wagon.

The dog cushioned the impact during the collision. It had a broken leg but was mostly just bruised all over.

"The baby, thank heaven," Aunt Callie said, rubbing the roundness of her stomach, "was just fine." She hesitated a moment, looking at Uncle Willie, then swallowed hard like she had a piece of biscuit stuck in her throat. "The doctors said that the dog cushioned the impact of the accident and saved the baby's life."

"So do you know what we named this sweet ole dog?" Uncle Willie asked, reaching for Aunt Callie's hand.

"Michael, of course, for the angel."

Where love is concerned,

an angel will do whatever it takes to get the job done.

Stranger on a Hillside

As the steep hillside shimmered before him in the rosy morning sunlight, Reece Hinton yelled and yanked hard on the reins he held in his calloused hands. Maneuvering mules and a wagon down this steep grade was bad enough in good weather, but today, with the roads completely covered in ice, it was next to impossible.

The mules whinnied, their warm breath as white as the snow-covered fields around them. Behind them loomed the wagonload of railroad ties they had been pulling since four o'clock this morning. Hinton, a strong and proud 75 years old, had cut and dressed the ties from his own forest and loaded them into the wagon himself.

Now, however, the old man regretted not bringing along one of his sons or grandsons to help him. If he tried going down that hill on his own, he might lose his wagon, his load, or his mules. At the least, he risked an accident if the mules couldn't find footing on the slick road. At worst, he risked putting himself and his animals in danger.

But he had gone too many miles to give up now. Besides, his family needed the money. Bowing his head and taking a deep breath, Hinton clenched his hands and hoped for the best. He would need every ounce of strength possible to keep his wagon from careening out of control on the way down the steep, slippery slope. Not enough brake action would invite a wild plunge. Too much could lock the wheels, jerking them sideways—and, at the edge of the road, there was a steep drop-off into a ravine. The

Sometimes we hear a soft voice, sending a message of hope and endurance. Remember angels are messengers from a place far beyond our own. We do well when we listen.

mules snorted and pawed the ground as if they were trying to tell him something.

Hinton spoke encouragingly to the protesting animals, then he clicked the reins. As they lunged, he jerked the wooden brake stick back and forth to maintain control.

Inch by inch, they moved forward. Then, though Hinton strived to control it, the wagon began gaining momentum. The mules fought in vain for footing on the slick ice. Hinton struggled with the brake. But between the ice and the down-slope and their rapidly increasing speed, he was quickly losing the battle. Hinton swallowed hard and squeezed his eyes closed, praying for a miracle. He wasn't much of a churchgoer, and he usually left the praying to his wife. But today he began to pray, silently at first, and then out loud like he was in a prayer meeting. "Help me, Lord!" he cried again and again, as if God were just over the next ridge.

Just then someone called, "Hey, mister, could you use a hand?"

Jerking around, Hinton saw a farmer leaning against the roadside fence. "Sure could," he yelled back, the panic evident in his voice as he fought with the brake stick while tugging on the reins.

In a moment, the stranger reached the wagon. "Can't blame you. This hill is almost impossible when it's iced up like this. Headed into town?"

"Right. Got to deliver this load of ties."

Hinton expected the farmer to help with the reins up front or pull back on the wagon from behind. He did neither. Instead, the stranger just put his hand on the wagon side and walked companionably alongside it in the snow. As soon as he touched the wagon, something remarkable happened. Instantly the mules steadied; the wagon stopped slipping and sliding. They could have been traveling on flat ground! When they finally reached a level stretch of road, the old man reached for his new friend's hand. "You'll never know how much I've appreciated your help." But there was no one there! Now that the danger had passed, the stranger was gone.

Hinton got down off the wagon to look for him, but he found no one. There weren't any footprints in the snow to explain where the man had come from or where he had disappeared to. He couldn't guess who the stranger might have been.

Hinton concluded, "If you need God's help, ask for it. If you're someone he doesn't hear from very often, be sure to speak up!"

Some believe angel wings are made of the prayers of children.

Wisdom Teeth

"When I grow up," my granddaughter Molly announced to her kindergarten class a few weeks ago, "I want to have a gold tooth like my Grandma Emily!"

I grinned widely at my reflection in the early morning mirror, admiring the gold crown on a back molar. It glinted and sparkled in the light like the reflection from an angel's halo.

I look like a middle-aged pirate, I thought to myself as I brushed and flossed. Yet, let me hasten to add, I say a prayer of thanksgiving every day for the toothache that saved my life.

I also pray each day that Molly and my other grandchildren will wind up being watched over by an angel like mine, the generous one who shared her love of chocolate with me that fateful day at work.

We were winding up a large project at the factory where I work. I supervise the packaging and shipping of computer parts all over the world. Most of the time, the workers are congenial and hardworking. But pressure can build up. A tight deadline was looming, and I was doing all I could to keep spirits up and tempers cool. Management was using fewer people to do more jobs, and I had to convince workers they could do it!

I was looking forward to my midmorning break. I always have a cup of hot tea and those chocolate cupcakes, which come packaged two to a set, from the vending machine. They seemed to soothe the stomachache I'd been having lately. Stress, I had diagnosed.

It didn't help that, first of all, all the cupcakes were gone. Then the machine jammed and wouldn't release the candy bar I wanted, although it kept my money. Glumly, I walked to my desk with just my tea. I decided to look through my desk drawers for some crackers.

On my desk, however, sat a small gift tin wrapped in shiny pink foil and tied with a big bow. There was no card, and no one claimed responsibility for leaving it. I had a secret pal who knew me well. Inside, nestled in foil cups, was my favorite candy of all time: homemade chocolate-covered buttery almond toffee. I had eaten four pieces by the time break was over.

I popped one last piece in my mouth on the way back to the assembly line. I bit down . . . right on a large piece of nutshell. A searing pain shot through my jaw as air hit the tooth I had broken.

Two pain relievers and several hours later, I finally went home. I put an ice pack on my jaw, took more pain relievers, and dabbed on over-the-counter tooth-numbing gel.

By midnight, I was aching all over. The tooth was obviously developing an abscess. The next morning I was sitting in the dentist's parking lot when he arrived. I told him about the gift of the candy.

"Some secret pal," he said, peering at my broken molar.

Whoever it was, though, was just trying to be friendly, no doubt, knowing how hard I was working to keep morale up.

"This temporary filling and packing should take care of you until we can get rid of the infection that's already started," the dentist said, sending me home with an antibiotic and pain medication.

Despite the dentist's ministrations, however, by midnight, the toothache was worse. I was also having a reaction to the antibiotic—I had a fever, chills, headache, nausea.

"Take me to the hospital," I said, waking my husband. All evening, "Go now, go now, go now," had played in my mind like a record stuck in a groove. "I can't stand this any longer."

"The cure is worse than the disease," I muttered to my husband as we

drove to the hospital. "It's like the old joke," I added, "if you have a headache, hit your thumb with a hammer and your head will stop hurting. It's a good theory, my stomach feels better."

I didn't need to explain very much once the emergency room staff saw how sick I was. I showed them my temporary filling, the culprit antibiotic, and the pain tablets. They popped me in a room quicker than you could say "Tooth

Fairy," and they called in the doctor. He promptly loaded me in a wheelchair and propelled me straight to surgery.

"Her gallbladder was within hours, if not minutes, of rupturing, spilling deadly toxins into her bloodstream," he told my husband a couple of hours later when I was in recovery.

I didn't know anything about this until later. As I was waking up in the recovery room, hazily coming out of the anesthetic, I carefully bit down on a piece of candy. I had been dreaming about the candy, I realized, since there was nothing in my mouth except the woozy taste of medicine. But all that night, the sense persisted that something buttery, something delicious and wonderful, was teasingly just out of my sight in the hands of a person I couldn't identify. Whoever it was stayed with me through the night, munching, munching, munching, until I finally drifted off into regular sleep.

I awoke to the smiling face of the surgeon leaning over me. "How are we doing?" he asked.

I groaned, rubbing my stomach. It was unfair, I complained a bit peevishly, that I had come in with a toothache and wound up with a bellyache.

"Ah," said the doctor in his best bedside manner, "the candy that cracked your tooth saved your life. Another few hours, and we would've been singing hymns at your funeral."

And it was then that I spied a small pile of crumpled foil candy cups on my windowsill and knew who had brought me the candy, an angel with a sweet tooth.

Silent Angels

Walking through the drugstore, I noticed the young salesclerk. Her name tag read "Darla," and I recognized her as the little girl I used to babysit many years before. I watched as she wrote a note to a customer. Darla had been born deaf, and this simple method (despite hours of signing and speaking training) seemed to be her preferred method of communicating with the public.

It must have been well over 20 years since "the event" had taken place. I thought of what could have been, of the tragedy that would have touched so many lives if things had turned out just slightly different.

At the hopeful and young age of about-to-turn 14, I had a thriving babysitting business. I was watching Darla and Billy during the summer months while their parents went to work. Darla had just had a birthday, and she'd gotten her first bike, a metallic blue number with high handle-bars and a banana seat. Darla thought she was the coolest thing on two wheels (or four, to be precise, since she still needed training wheels), and I loved watching the joy on her pretty face as she rode her new gift.

Darla's father had insisted that she ride the bike in the driveway unless he was with her. As he signed this to her, she moaned and turned away— the typical response when she didn't want to "see" what you were saying.

"I'll watch her," I promised. "I won't let her out in the street."

He looked worried, but he nodded his approval and left for work.

Darla's brother, Billy, who was jealous of all the attention his sister was getting, was in the yard doing somersaults and cartwheels, desperately trying to draw me to him. Darla rode her bike in the large driveway, circling proudly, waving each time she passed.

Then I heard the squealing tires of a car speeding into the subdivision. They say that a plane crash occurs when more than one probable calamity occurs at the same time. In a similar vein, our small world seemed about to crash.

First, Billy fell doing a cartwheel and hit his head on a brick. He started crying, and a small stream of blood that ran down the side of his face sent him into hysterics. Darla, unable to hear the sounds of her brother crying or the car speeding in our direction, decided at that moment to try out her new bike in the street. Too late to stop her, I could only watch, my heart pounding so hard it hurt, as she sped out of the driveway. The car was coming closer and closer, and I was powerless to do anything.

Picking up Billy, I ran after Darla, but I did not stand a chance—she had too much of a lead on me. As soon as I saw the car, its driver also saw Darla, who was now in the middle of the street, pedaling and looking up at a small flock of starlings flying overhead. The driver honked and yelled at her, but he did not slow down. In an instant Darla was going to be hit.

"She's deaf! Stop!" I screamed at the car, but the music was up so high that the driver couldn't hear me.

I screamed at Darla to stop, then I shielded Billy's eyes from what I knew was going to be a horrible scene.

The car flew past me. The driver finally realized that Darla was not going to move in time, so he tried to stop. His brakes screeched, and his front end started to turn as he began sliding sideways down the pavement. The tires smoked, but he couldn't stop the heavy vehicle at that speed.

At just the right moment, one bird from the flock of starlings swooped down in front of Darla and landed in a tree to the side of the road. Darla followed its flight and turned her bike, pedaling to the tree for a closer look. The car, now almost fully sideways, slid behind her, barely missing the back of her bike. Darla stared happily at the bird, never seeing the car that had almost taken her life. The driver swore at her and sped away. But at least she was safe.

That moment, at the impressionable age of almost 14, I began to believe in God and angels and spirits and everything else that rescues small children from certain death. For years I thought about that tiny bird and why it flew to the tree at that exact moment, leaving its fellow travelers to fly on. It confirmed that even the smallest of things can change your life.

A tear ran down my cheek as I stood in the bright, orderly drugstore, thinking about all the tiny, yet profound crossroads in our lives—many of which we're not even aware of. How thankful I was that God sent a angel in the form of a starling to save that little girl's life. I could only imagine what other miracles I'd never even noticed! Surely he puts us where we need to be exactly when we need to be there. Darla finished helping another customer, and I walked over to say hello.

No Exit

I waited for the answering service to connect the caller. Crisis-line volunteers never answer directly. Rarely did we talk to a client more than once or twice, so I was surprised when I recognized the voice on the other end of the line. It was Denise, a young woman I'd spoken to a couple of times in the past. Both times she'd been badly beaten by her husband, and both times I'd encouraged her to go to the women's shelter to avoid further abuse.

"I can't leave him," she'd said. "I have to stay."

When I heard her voice this time, I felt a mixture of relief and concern. At least she was not in a hospital or, worse yet, the morgue. She was probably calling again after yet another beating.

I carried the phone to the kitchen and poured a cup of coffee as I listened.

"I'm so glad it's you," she said, when I introduced myself. "I really just called because I hoped they could get a message to you. I wanted to tell you about a strange thing that happened."

"Strange" was not how I'd have described her past beatings, and she wasn't whispering as abuse victims often do. Something must have happened.

Denise didn't wait for my response. "Remember I told you that our office was moving downtown, and that Dan had wanted me to quit when he heard. He was so jealous because I'd be meeting new people."

"Well," she went on, "last Friday I agreed to work late to get the office set up. Everyone else had already left when I finished. I hurried to collect my things and head home. I dreaded facing Dan's accusations that I'd just been out playing around with some other man."

Why, I wondered, did abusive spouses always seem obsessed with the idea that their partners were cheating?

"Anyway," Denise continued, "when I went downstairs to go through the main entrance, it was locked...chained shut from the inside. I wasn't worried at first. After all, a big office building like that had to have lots of exits."

While Denise talked, I recorded her information on the crisis call form.

"I checked the door at the end of the nearest hall," she said. "There was a sign that said 'No Exit.' I tried it anyway, but it wouldn't open. I checked several other doors. Each had a 'No Exit' sign. By then I was getting panicked. I could just imagine the punishment Dan would have in store for me for being so late."

I could imagine it too...and the longer it took for her to get home, the worse the beating would probably be.

Denise went on. "I was nearly frantic by then, running furiously back and forth. I spotted a fire escape and rushed to it. Once more I was met by a 'No Exit' sign. The fine print explained that in case of fire, all the fire doors would automatically open."

Poor Denise. I understood her fear and frustration.

"By then," she said, "I was terrified. I ran back to the front door and began banging on it. 'Get me out of here,' I yelled. I thought maybe somebody outside would hear me, though I don't know what I thought they'd do. Then I realized someone was behind me. I turned quickly around. An elderly man was standing there. I was sobbing by then," Denise said, "and I explained that there was no way out."

"There's always a way out," he said reassuringly. "Just follow me."

"I followed him through the dark hall to a door I'd not noticed before. It was locked just like the others, but my rescuer reached into the pocket of his overalls and pulled out the key. He unlocked the door. I thanked him and hurried to my car. I still hated to think what would happen when I got home. I got my cell phone out of the glove compartment to call Dan, but even as I dialed our number I thought of the man's words: 'There's always a way out.' I remembered you'd said that, too, when you gave me the number for the women's shelter. I still had the number in my purse. Instead of calling Dan, I called the shelter. That's where I am now."

I breathed a sigh of relief. She was safe! "Thank heavens for the night custodian," I said.

Denise laughed. "That's what I thought, too, until the next day when I brought him a thank-you card. I asked the receptionist to give it to him. She looked at me strangely and told me there was no night custodian."

As I hung up from our conversation, I thought about the night custodian. There may be no night custodian, but there most certainly was a night guardian watching over Denise—complete with invisible angel wings!

Just Passing By

Bundled in raincoat and tall rubber boots, Kathy carried in jugs of bottled water, kerosene for the heater, and batteries for the generator from the station wagon. It had started to storm while she had been in town getting emergency supplies. When you lived in the country, you did such things automatically.

"We'd better be prepared," she told the tabby cat, Orphan Annie. Who knew how long the power would stay on, she thought, if the winds took down the power lines. Spring had come in like a lion and showed no signs of being tamed.

Instead of turning on the furnace, Kathy decided to light a small fire in the fireplace to take the chill from the room. She carried in logs from the front porch where they were stored underneath a tarpaulin.

With the cat sniffing each log for remembrances of the small woodland critters that had last scampered over them, Kathy stacked the logs and kindling beside the hearth. When she was finished, she added a few to the already blazing fire. They were apple and brought a soft, fragrant aroma into the room.

Kathy settled herself on the couch with a cup of lemon spice tea, the cat, and stacks of the car advertisement sections from area newspapers. Thanks to her husband, she also had reams of car buyers' information papers from the Internet that he had printed out for her before he left on a business trip earlier in the week. And while she had been out shopping on her way home from work today, Kathy had bought several car guide magazines. She needed a new car.

Her heart, however, wasn't in the search.

It wasn't just a matter of money, although finances were always a major consideration. It was a matter of sentiment. Of connection to something—someone—special.

That was why, to the amusement and bewilderment of family and coworkers who teased her unmercifully about her battered green station wagon with its decided "list" to one side and already rusting fenders, Kathy had kept it all winter. She was even fond of the raspy, scraping sound the car made when she hit even the smallest bump causing the frame to hit the fender. It added a percussive note to her life, she thought. A jaunty note—a kind of "Hallelujah" chorus all its own. She smiled at the thought.

Each time Kathy passed the car in the garage, driveway, or parking lot, she would pat its crumpled side with the affection usually reserved for very good friends.

It was in the confines of the car that she had met someone even more special.

Six months earlier, during a winter blizzard, Kathy's car had spun off the icy road in a series of graceful pirouettes and had come to rest in a deep snow-filled ditch.

How quickly it had happened.

Fortunately, she realized taking stock as she tried to control the spinning car, there were no other cars around to get tangled up with.

That's good news and bad news, she told herself, for no one would likely be coming this way for hours. Kathy's usual route, this winding stretch of blacktop, was a shortcut on country back roads between her house in a rural area of Vermont and the courthouse in town where she was a circuit court judge.

Used to weighing the facts and options of each situation, Kathy knew this one was not good: First, the pressure on her chest from the steering wheel where she was jammed would kill her if the sub-zero temperature didn't do it first. Fact number two: The airbag had deflated as quickly as it expanded and was threatening to suffocate her. No matter how she wriggled, she couldn't move enough to reach her cell phone to call for help: bad news number three.

She didn't have breath enough to sob aloud, but, in her mind, she was silently wailing like the lost child she had become. She had no idea how long it had been since the accident, but she knew that the deepening lethargy creeping through her body was a warning that she was about to lose consciousness. She drifted in and out of awareness, so cold now that she could no longer shiver.

Suddenly, with a warmth that belied the weather, a man, ordinary looking in denim coveralls and hooded parka, appeared beside her car.

He rubbed away the frost from her window. "Are you OK, lady?" he asked.

She peered up at him, grateful tears beginning to run down her cheeks. She could only nod, not having enough lung room to inhale deeply enough for a shout.

"We'll have you out of there in a minute," he said.

Before she could whisper, "Thank you," he disappeared.

She didn't see him return but heard a noise behind her. Glancing up in the rearview mirror, she saw him shoveling snow away from the exhaust. Of course. The carbon monoxide would have killed her even before the cold or the steering wheel's pressure.

Whether or not it was her imagination, she felt like she could breath easier, the air cleaner. She took little breaths, watching the tiny little puffs her shallow exhalations made in the frigid air.

"Sit still, now," the man said, shouting through the back window. "I'm going to be making some noise."

And, with that, she heard a wrenching sound as the rear station wagon door reluctantly opened. The man crawled in and appeared behind her.

Carefully, he lowered the car's seat back and helped her slide out to safety. He held her in his arms and let her take in several deep breaths.

"We've got to keep moving," he said.

It was only then, looking beyond him, that Kathy saw that she was within a few feet of a sharp drop-off down to the half-frozen river below. Add drowning to my list of means of death, she thought to herself, feeling near-hysterical laughter catching in her throat.

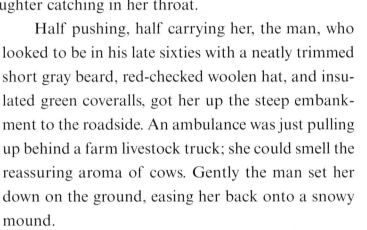

Half pushing, half carrying her, the man, who looked to be in his late sixties with a neatly trimmed short gray beard, red-checked woolen hat, and insulated green coveralls, got her up the steep embankment to the roadside. An ambulance was just pulling up behind a farm livestock truck; she could smell the reassuring aroma of cows. Gently the man set her down on the ground, easing her back onto a snowy mound.

The EMTs jumped from the ambulance, bringing a blanket and rescue equipment.

"I'm so glad he called you," Kathy said to the EMT who was gently stabilizing and strapping her onto the stretcher.

"Who?" said the EMT, looking around in confusion. "Nobody called. We were dispatched to another accident when we got the signal to disregard it. We just happened to be passing by."

When Kathy's husband went to the accident scene later that morning, there were no footprints other than hers climbing from the ditch, no tire tracks or other trace of a guardian angel who'd worn a red-checked hat and who drove a stock truck.

James

y friend James was drafted into the Army in 1969. He thought he could avoid the invitation to serve because he was enrolled at the local community college. Unfortunately, his plan didn't work. He apparently was not carrying a "full load," according to Uncle Sam, who was looking for employees to fill the positions available in Vietnam.

James was not a particularly religious person, and spirituality was definitely not part of his daily regimen. He was rebellious and headstrong. However, he resigned himself to the fact that he had been drafted and went along with what he was told to do.

James left for basic training on September 19, 1969. As always, he hid his fear of the unknown with belligerence. He was not one to call on God, angels, or any kind of higher power. He believed that he needed nothing or no one but himself.

I had known James for seven years prior to his departure. I knew he'd had a difficult upbringing filled with physical abuse and emotional deprivation, culminating with the suicide of his father. He was a person of few words, and he tended to believe that his whole life was a bad luck story. In fact, he often used the old cliché, "If it wasn't for bad luck, I wouldn't have any luck at all." To say he was cynical would be an understatement.

He returned from basic training in time for Christmas, and, soon after that, he received his orders for overseas duty. He knew that his stopover in Thailand would be just a stepping stone before he was shipped out to Vietnam.

I'm not sure which one of us was more upset about this turn of events. Neither of us spoke much about it. We didn't talk about the distance or the fear or the safety factor or that he was going to war and might not return.

My most treasured possession at the time was a medal my grandmother had given me when I was 12 years old. It was small and gold, the size of a dime, with a baptismal scene on one side. I wore it, always, on a chain around my neck. It had been purchased by one of my grandmother's friends while she was visiting the Vatican in Rome. The medal was especially important to me because it had been blessed by Pope John XXIII, a gentle soul with a kind face who was loved by many people around the world.

Before James left for his overseas assignment, I gave him my precious medal. I told him to wear it always and said it would help to bring him home safely. He thanked me but didn't show much emotion. My guess was that he thought it was a rather simple plan—thinking that something hanging around his neck would protect him from anything, especially bullets or bombs. But he wore it anyway.

One night, while he was in Vietnam, I had a dream that was so vivid and real I woke up in a sweat. During the dream I was asleep yet awake. My body was floating over my bed, and I was looking over a rise. There was gunfire all around, and I spotted James. He was not in his usual place, driving heavy equipment. I had always found it reassuring to know that

he was on an earthmover, which put tons of steel between him and any land mine he might hit.

I didn't know how he happened to be on foot now, clutching his weapon and heading over the rise. He continued to move forward, and I could not see if anyone else was around him until I spotted a few Vietnamese civilians in the bushes ahead of him. One had a rifle and the other was reaching into his loose shirt.

In horror, I began calling out to James. I was screaming at him, yet I could not hear my own voice. I yelled again and again until he finally looked back, in search of something. As he did, he tripped and fell backward, rolling down the hill. At that moment he became a target for Vietnamese gunfire. He rolled down and away as a grenade exploded in the spot where he had just been. I watched this scene as it unfolded in slow motion before my dreaming, open eyes.

I woke with no voice. My eyes were wide open in disbelief, and my mouth was parched. I did not dare call his mother to tell her about my dream. I knew I'd be informed if something terrible happened.

James returned to the United States shortly after that. He had received the Purple Heart, which he threw away before coming home. I knew James had seen action in Vietnam, but he never discussed what took place during his tour of duty. He kept everything to himself and always said he did not want to talk about it. I wondered why he chose not to seek the counsel of a therapist or a spiritual advisor to help him sort through the rubble in his mind. I know the scars were deep and the horrors were many.

It wasn't until 25 years later that I dared talk to him about his experiences. One day I finally asked James if he remembered, during the war, being called while he was running up a hill with a rifle in his hand. He

looked at me and said yes. He remembered. Someone screamed his name, and he fell down the hill after losing his footing. He wasn't sure if he would survive the attack, and he didn't know how he ended up in the hospital.

He was dumbfounded to realize that I knew of "the hill" without him telling me. I took a deep breath and told him about my dream.

James still had the medal I'd given him 25 years before. He held it with his thumb and forefinger while we spoke. The medal had an angel on it, holding an infant who was being baptized. Could he have been that infant, held by an angel, getting baptized into the belief of something higher than himself?

His mind was suddenly spinning. Could he possibly have a guardian angel who watched over him? An angel who had worked through me to protect him? Could there be any other answer? There didn't seem to be any. He had been in danger all those years ago, in that strange faraway

land, in the midst of a battleground. He wasn't able to save himself, so his guardian angel had taken over.

The more James thought about the turn of events on the hill that day, the more he realized that what he had was not good luck or bad luck. It was the protection and divine intervention of something bigger than him—much bigger. He knows it wasn't the medal that saved his life in Vietnam, but he wears it as a reminder of how God's angels carried him to safety during the war.

James still does not talk about Vietnam or his experiences there. But ever since the day I told him about my dream, he will talk about one thing: how he believes that he's alive today because his guardian angel was with him on that hill. Maybe it's true that he was at the right place at the right time—or maybe his guardian angel was.

Sometimes the truth that we are not alone is a rope that keeps us from slipping, much as the rope a climber clings to on the side of a mountain.

Comforting Angels

Because they've seen a better place, angels whisper hope to us in our darkest moments.

Closer and Closure

I eased uncomfortably around the display of rakes at the end of the aisle. Tools. Appliances. Hardware. A man's domain.

I eyed the display of shiny metal knobs, hinges, and screws. Replacement parts.

But where is the replacement for Daddy? What can patch the gaping hole in my heart?

"Can I help you, ma'am?" Brushing a hand over his fringe of cotton-wool hair, the clerk looked up. "Say, aren't you one of Mac's daughters?"

I nodded.

"Sorry I couldn't make it to his funeral. Sure will miss him around here. He liked to stop in and shoot the breeze, you know."

I knew.

Daddy loved people: spending time with them, chatting with them, helping them. "Say, don't think I'm weird or anything. But Mac came to me in a dream the other night."

I lowered my eyes.

He cleared his throat, glanced away, and reached out a scarred hand to straighten the pocketknife display. "Yea, well, sure will miss him around here."

Why had I gone to the hardware store, I wondered hours later as I drove back to Colorado. Closure? Or was the better word "closer"? Maybe to feel near Daddy one more time by prowling another of his old haunts?

Comforting Angels

My dad's unexpected death three months earlier still had me reeling and feeling fragmented, even incomplete. I had tried to comfort Mother, sort out their affairs, and see to my four teenagers a state away.

Now I felt a new emotion creeping in: jealousy. Envy that a near stranger had dreamed about my daddy, had felt close to him.

Why not me, God? I just need—something. Anything. A second chance to thank him, to tell him how much I love him, to say a final goodbye.

Blinking away treacherous tears, I sniffed, steadied the steering wheel, and turned the black knob on the car radio, searching for music. I needed it to keep me alert on the long and lonely trip home. An oldies station played "Goodnight Sweetheart," and I sang along. "...although I'm not beside you...still my love will guide you...." I choked out the words.

I want him back, God. I need him to be part of my life.

The next week, I tried piecing together my old routine. Immediately I reclaimed my long-time volunteer work at a local nursing home. Although I hadn't inherited his talent, I certainly had acquired Daddy's love of music—and the powerful desire to share it. Playing the piano and leading the music on Wednesdays in a casual sing-along never failed to lift my spirits. A genuine love for each of the elderly residents at the home brought joy to my life.

However, there were some songs I avoided. Songs I had heard over and over and over again until the words were imprinted in both my mind and my heart.

Songs like "Green Grow the Lilacs," "Now Is the Hour," or "Moon River." And, of course, there was Daddy's all-time favorite—the hauntingly

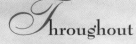

Throughout history angels have been our connection to heaven. There seems to be no protocol too fine or too unworthy for heaven's angels to touch down and offer their guiding light.

tender "Danny Boy." Those songs reminded me of him serenading us during the lazy Sunday afternoon car rides of my youth. Songs that painted powerful portraits of Daddy with one or another of his eclectic collection of instruments—the harmonica, the guitar, the keyboard, the Jew's harp, and the dulcimer.

Those memories are tender and precious.

So I surprised myself that day at the nursing home when I pulled out the dog-eared sheet music for one of Daddy's more rollicking choices, "Shoo-fly Pie." My fingers flicked out the light melody.

"Do any of you recognize this one?" I began to sing. "Shoo-fly pie, and apple pan dowdy, makes your eyes light up...."

Falteringly, age-rusted voices joined mine. Their words rattled like a collection of corroded screws in a shabby cigar box. But as creaking memories hinged open, their voices gained strength.

And then I heard it: Daddy accompanying me on his harmonica. The lively strains, the breathy notes, even his upper and lower dentures clacking a syncopated rhythm all their own against the shiny metal of his best "mouth organ."

His presence was real. Tangible.

I could *feel* him standing right behind me. He was *with* me. He was *part* of me.

Eyes swimming, voice cracking, I finished the song. Wrists limp, I paused to let the merry music wash over me, to save and savor the last lingering notes still in the air, to preserve the sacredness of both the moment and the memory.

194

Then I swiveled around on the walnut piano bench and . . . came face-to-harmonica with matted haired, pajama-clad Paul.

The snaggle-toothed new resident grinned and wheeled closer. Broad farm fingers fumbled with an oversize red harmonica. A trembling hand tapped out the spit against the flannel on his thigh.

"How's about we try 'Oh, Susannah' next?" Paul cackled and lifted the harmonica to his dry, cracked lips.

Swiping at my damp cheeks, I took a deep breath, closed the sheet music, and put it beside me on the bench. Mechanically, I selected a songbook and ran my index finger down the table of contents.

Huh. So much for a touching, spiritual moment.

Deflated, I glanced around the wheelchair-lined room where aged human beings—dented and scarred—were parked bumper-to-knee like tired taxicabs waiting at a busy airport.

There was blind Alma. And well-groomed Irene. And Eleanor-who-was-crippled.

Across the room I saw Jim and Hazel and Gladys-in-pain. The next row included Anna-the-smiler, Leona-the-whistler, Dora and Ava . . . . The people I loved.

And all of them waiting patiently, expectantly for me to begin the next song. Any song that would lift their spirits and, for a brief span of time,

enable them to transcend reality to a gentler season in their memories and in their lives.

Please, let these moments take them closer to their own loved ones.

Then, I smiled—inside and out—right into Paul's beaming face.

And, thank you, God, for sending this grizzled angel to teach me a lesson about legacy and love!

"'Oh, Susannah' is a perfect choice, Paul." I patted his leg. "Your harmonica playing adds a lot. I'm so glad you're here with us today." I was not surprised at all to realize I genuinely meant it. Taking a cleansing breath, I grinned around the room.

"I'm sure each and every one of you will recognize this next melody. Ready everyone? All together now!"

So we made music together: Paul with his harmonica and me with my piano; all of us singing and winging our way through the sunny autumn afternoon. And I knew then that I didn't need a momentary sign, or vision, or dream. Daddy was a permanent part of my life. He was as much a part of each note as he was a part of me. Music brought him closer to me. That was better than a final good-bye.

For the last song that day I chose "Danny Boy." My daddy's favorite.

A Cherished Angel

*O*ur family has always cherished Grandma Madge. She was a special lady with a knack for helping friends and family members when they needed it. Madge was always the first person to take a home-cooked meal to someone who was sick. The treasured time she spent with them even surpassed the healing benefit of her famous German dumplings.

That's why it seemed sadly ironic that, now, friends and family sat at *her* bedside. When Madge learned about her fatal illness, she'd insisted on staying home. "To be surrounded by my angel collection," she beamed.

Madge's colossal collection of angels—1,500 to be exact—had started with just a few Christmas tree ornaments and occasional figurines she picked up at souvenir shops or garage sales. But it didn't take long for her sons to discover that contributions to Madge's plethora of angels were the perfect solution to the what-to-get-Mom dilemma. Soon every friend, neighbor, grandchild, and in-law bought her an angel for every holiday, birthday, and anniversary. It wasn't long before her tiny cottage overflowed with a host of heavenly beings.

She proudly displayed many of them year-round on shelves, the coffee table, end tables, and on top of the TV. In the guestroom, she assembled a choir of angels—she reserved that room for musical figurines. Hundreds of singing, twirling, dancing angels crowded antique shelves, hutches, and bedside stands.

Each year on the first day of November, Madge began the month-long process of bringing out the rest of her collection. Angels graced her Christmas tree and the floor beneath it, then cascaded everywhere, from the buffet, to the mantel, to the bathroom sink—to the top of the refrigerator! To Madge, each angel was a reminder of a special person who loved her. She inscribed the name of the giver on the bottom of each angel, along with the date she had received it. She gave explicit directions: "When I pass through the Pearly Gates, make sure every angel goes back to the person who gave it to me."

Now, with a hospice nurse and Madge's two sisters staying with her, that loving task seemed imminent. Her grandson, Troy, stopped by to spend some precious time with his grandma. Sitting on the edge of the bed, he tenderly caressed her hand. "You've been an angel to us all, Grandma—a true gift from God." Troy was the last person to visit his Grandma Madge. A few hours after he left, she entered through those Pearly Gates.

Her sisters, Renee and Gladys, and the hospice nurse gathered in the living room, marveling at how Madge had died with the same dignity, courage, and grace with which she had lived. A faint melody interrupted their discussion. Bewildered, they turned their heads, trying to discover the source of the music. As they crept toward the guest bedroom, the tune grew louder. There, on a table, one lone angel played the song "Cherish" from beginning to end. Then it stopped. With trembling hands, Gladys picked it up and read, "From Troy, 1992." Gladys held the figurine to her chest. "Thanks, Madge, for letting us know you've joined God's heavenly collection of angels."

"Our angel," Renee whispered, "returned to the Giver."

Hush! my dear, lie still and slumber,
Holy angels guard thy bed!
Heavenly blessings without number
Gently falling on thy head.

—Isaac Watts

The Love of His Gift

Angels appear to us in times of sorrow and grief to help us mend our broken hearts. After hearing my father's story, I am convinced of it.

I have many fond childhood memories and consider myself very lucky to have been raised by two special parents. Mom and Dad were totally devoted to one another; she was the love of his life. They raised their three daughters with warmth and humor, and they gave us a home filled with love and security.

My mother battled emphysema, and during the last two years of her life she was confined to a respirator. Dad was always there for her, and as she became ill their roles gradually reversed. He did the shopping, cooking, and cleaning, caring for Mom as she had done for him all the years prior. He never complained and seemed happy for the chance to care for his beloved wife. One night, she died peacefully in her sleep.

My sisters and I tried to comfort Dad as we all mourned together. A few days after Mom died, Dad said to us, "You know, I've never been alone. I went from home to college, into the Navy, then I married your mother. This is the first time I've been on my own." He was 73 years old. He missed her terribly, the love of his life.

The city my folks lived in had a music and crafts festival along the main street every year. My parents had always enjoyed this event—strolling the streets, enjoying the music, viewing the art displays, and delighting in the general air of friendliness and fun. Once again, the festival was scheduled, but dad wondered if he'd enjoy it alone. He decided he needed to get out and mingle with people to combat his grief and take his mind away from the solitary life he was now experiencing.

The day of the festival, Dad walked up and down the crowded streets, enjoying the sights, sounds, and smells, but as the heat intensified he found himself getting a little weary. He began to look for a sidewalk café where he could sip some lemonade and catch his breath.

He heard a voice call out to him, "Excuse me, sir, would you like to sit down?" He turned to find a pretty young woman smiling and motioning to a chair next to hers.

He graciously accepted her offer, and they began talking about the fair, the weather, and other general things that strangers chat about.

As Dad and the young lady conversed, she asked if he was married. He smiled sadly and began reminiscing about Mother. His sorrow and sense of loss were apparent, and the young lady listened attentively. As Dad relayed the story to me later, he remarked how surprised he was that "a pretty young thing would let an old codger bend her ear." Surely, he thought, she would have preferred doing something a bit more fun!

After chatting a while, the young lady smiled and reached into a shopping bag that was sitting by her feet. She presented my dad with a gift, saying, "I bought this for myself because I collect angels, but I'd be delighted if you would accept this. I believe it was intended for you." In her hands was a small porcelain angel, sitting and mending a broken heart.

As my dad recounted this story to me a few days later, we both realized that theirs had not been a chance meeting. An angel had entered Dad's world with a gift to heal his broken heart.

Dad passed on not long after that encounter. He had played a round of golf (his "second love") and, as usual, topped it off with an afternoon nap. He passed away in his sleep, and his heart was finally mended as he rejoined my mother, the love of his life.

As for that angel with the broken heart . . . it's my most valued possession.

A Hug From Heaven

Everyone goes through a grieving period sometime in their life. It's inevitable, but that doesn't make it any less painful.

Sarah was my first grandchild, born to my oldest daughter, Kathy, and her husband, Eric. I don't think I've ever been more delighted in my life as I was the day Sarah was born. She had a personality and understanding that seemed to make her older than her years, and when the family gathered, she was always the center of attention. I must say, I loved her dearly.

Shortly after her fifth birthday, Sarah started showing signs of increased fatigue and being easily irritated. My daughter took her to the doctor, and they assured her that she was fine. But her health didn't improve. The weekend just before Father's Day, Sarah's worried parents took her to the Children's Hospital in Buffalo. She died there two days later from a viral infection that had settled in her heart.

I don't think I have ever experienced such overwhelming grief as I did over the loss of that child. I just couldn't let her go. Even after a year had passed, I still had trouble getting to sleep at night. I would toss and turn and think of how I had never given Sarah one last hug. I prayed to God every night, asking for one last chance to see her again and maybe hug her one more time.

One night after falling asleep, a voice called out to me and said, "Ted, look who's here." Up in the corner of a white room was a figure I saw only from the shoulders up. The person had short brown hair and a smiling face I didn't recognize. This angelic figure pointed toward a doorway, and, as I turned my head, I could see a little girl with long brown hair standing in front of a mirror. I immediately knew who it was and called out, "Sarah!" She turned and smiled, then ran toward me yelling, "Grandpa!" She put her arms around me and squeezed me tight around my neck, giving me the biggest hug I've ever had. It was so real, as if she were still alive and her death had been a bad dream. I never wanted to let go—I just wanted to keep my arms around her forever.

Just as quickly as she appeared in my dream, she left. But I woke up knowing that I had finally gotten my hug from heaven.

Light as a feather and quieter than snow,
your angel flits and flurries through your life,
engaged in all your concerns.

Angel in the Air

I'd gone to Paris on business against my wife's wishes. "You won't make it home for our daughter's birthday," she'd told me angrily, "and this is the second time you've missed it!"

But there was also the matter of landing this top account. So I'd compromised and left the meeting a day early. I'd make it home for the birthday this year, I vowed.

Traffic was heavy on the way to the airport, but, thanks to the gutsy driving of a French cabby, I made it to the gate in time. I folded my 6′4″ frame into my comfortable first-class seat with minutes to spare. I had just opened my newspaper when the flight attendant interrupted.

"I'm so sorry, sir," she began, "I know this is the seat assigned to you. But we've experienced a mix-up in reservations," she continued awkwardly, "and one of our other passengers has a critical need for this seat."

I frowned. "I, too, have a need for it," I snapped. "I pay for first class because I just don't fit well back there!" I indicated the cramped conditions in coach. "I'm sure there's someone else you can move," I added, looking pointedly at the greasy-haired man with the tattoo sitting across the aisle.

"Sorry, sir. But we need your seat for his bodyguard. That's JG, the rock star. The airline will give you a full refund and a free seat today in coach, unless you'd rather wait for a first-class seat on tomorrow's plane?"

Another day in Paris wouldn't hurt me—at least not until I tried to walk into my house after my daughter had already blown out her candles.

I tried once again to argue, but, even as I added that I was claustrophobic, the flight attendant simply folded my paper and reached for my briefcase in the overhead bin.

"If you'll just follow me, sir," she cooed.

I trudged behind her, banging against the tightly packed seats as I made my way awkwardly down the narrow aisle.

"Here!" the attendant said brightly, "at least it's an aisle seat, to accommodate your long legs," she pointed to a narrow seat next to a small, white-haired woman reading a paperback.

I let out a sigh. What I wouldn't do for my daughter. As I squeezed into the small space between rows, inadvertently pulling the hair of the woman in front of me as I awkwardly tried to position my body to lower it into the small seat, I hoped my wife could appreciate my sacrifice. My knees pressed against the back of the seat in front of me, drawing an angry response from the woman whose hair I'd just pulled.

I hadn't lied about being claustrophobic, though it usually wasn't too bad. But the close quarters back here made me break out in a cold sweat. I leaned my head back against the seat and closed my eyes. I was weary at the beginning, and now I was also cramped and nervous, and it could only get worse. The rather pleasing sense of martyrdom I'd briefly experienced began to turn to bitterness and anger at the prospect of facing 13 hours in this position. I didn't know who I resented more for getting me in this predicament: my wife, the flight attendant, the rock star, everyone in coach who made it so crowded in here, the airlines for cramming us in like sardines, the first-class passengers who were relaxing in comfort. At least making my "enemies list" took the edge off the claustrophobia.

I tried to breathe deeply, and I glanced at my neighbor. She hadn't so much as glanced up from her book during my ordeal, though I'm sure I'd bumped her shoulder at least twice.

The plane taxied out and began its takeoff; I closed my eyes and tried to picture wide-open spaces. I hoped there would soon be a good movie to distract me.

The plane had not yet leveled off when I heard a noise and felt a vibration running under my feet. I opened my eyes and looked around. Several people around me were also looking around worriedly.

Then the captain's voice came over the loudspeaker, first in French, then in English: *"S'il vous plait, toutes les . . . ."* Will all flight attendants come forward to the cabin immediately."

When they returned, the flight attendants looked shaken, but they fanned out to cover all sections of the plane.

"There's nothing to be concerned about," our attendant said, trying valiantly to hide her own concern. "The captain is about to make an announcement."

Then the captain was speaking: "*Mesdames et Messieurs, je regrette* that we've lost an engine. But don't worry, we still have three more. We have to return to Paris, but first we need to cruise around up here for about an hour to get rid of some fuel. Listen very carefully to the instructions that the flight attendants give you to prepare you for landing."

Voices rose in concern in a babble of languages: Lost an engine? Did it drop off? Can we land safely?

Questions buzzed around us, but the flight attendant captured our attention when she said, "I am going to give you instructions now, and we will need to practice for a possible crash landing."

She then explained that we would need to take off our shoes and eye-glasses, lean over as far as we could, wrap our arms around our legs, and tuck our heads down. Then she pointed out all the exits and told us that, in the unlikely event there was a problem, we would use the chutes: "You'll cross your arms over your chest and jump feet first into the chute. Someone will be at the bottom to help."

Around the cabin I could hear some people crying, but most were surprisingly quiet. Everyone looked strained and worried.

My heart began to beat rapidly in my throat as I considered an hour of flying in circles stuck in this crowded cabin full of fear. And I was scared. The faces of my wife and daughter passed before me as my heart began to race, my scalp crawled, and I began to gasp for breath. A feeling of panic threatened to overwhelm me, and I knew I had to get up. As I began to stand, I felt a hand on my arm. It was a light touch, but it forced me back into my seat and held me there softly.

Bungling, blundering, feeling so alone, we struggle through some days only to find when the fog has lifted we are just where we should be—in the company of angels.

"This is certainly going to be an inconvenience," the little grand-motherly person began, "but the airlines will have to put us up in hotels overnight and feed us dinner and breakfast." She smiled delightedly. "Another evening in Paris, what luck!"

As I turned, incredulous, to face her, I found myself looking into the bluest eyes I'd ever seen. They were as clear as a young girl's, yet they were full of ageless wisdom and peace and contentment.

"I . . . can't . . . breathe!" I wheezed.

"There, there," she patted my arm and laid a cool hand on my fore-head, like my mother used to do when I was a kid. My heart slowed to nor-mal, and my breathing relaxed.

I admitted I was worried, and worse, that I was feeling claustrophobic.

"I'm not a bit worried," she said, taking my hand. "I just have this feeling that everything will work out just fine and that you'll get home just in time!"

I frowned, puzzled, but she went on, "I'm going on a world tour," she told me. "Where are you heading, actually?"

I told her, then I confessed about my daughter's party, my wife's con-cern that I wouldn't be there, and now mine that "I might not . . . even . . . ." I started to choke up.

"Oh!" She waived her hand as though she could brush away all my worries. "You won't even be late!" she predicted.

"You see," she began confidently, "I know this type of plane very well, it's an L-1011, which is considered by everyone to be a very good plane. My brother used to fly on them all the time."

"Well," I said, smiling and beginning to relax, "if it's so darn good, why'd it lose an engine?"

She laughed, and the sound reminded me of a fountain. "There, you see, it's so good that it can fly just fine with only three!"

I grinned and, oddly enough, believed her.

We passed the hour chatting nonstop, and she never let go of my hand. She was full of questions about everything and very excited about her upcoming trip. She smiled at others around us and drew them into our conversation.

I'd almost forgotten about our predicament, when the captain cut in.

"We're beginning our approach, and, unfortunately, we have another small problem—a flat tire. But we have plenty of other tires that are good, as well as three good engines. They know about our problem at the airport, and they have aid waiting for us, but I don't think we'll need any," he added.

"He's right, you know, we won't," said the little grandmother. "I have confidence in our pilot. And in our Shepherd," she said, raising her eyes toward heaven.

"Now," said the pilot, "as we get ready to touch down, I will count down from ten to one. When I get to one, I want you to assume the position and stay there. TEN, NINE, EIGHT...."

There was muffled crying and sobbing during the countdown, especially when the flight attendants buckled themselves into their seats and assumed the position.

"...THREE, TWO, ONE."

The rest of us followed suit, and, as the plane met the earth, there was a big jolt and roughness that seemed to go on forever. Then, miraculously, the plane came to a stop.

"Ladies and gentlemen, I give you Paris!" said the captain, with a big sigh. A cheer went up in the cabin.

"It was such a good landing, they didn't even have to use the chutes," I told my wife when I got home the next evening. Thank God I was in coach, sitting beside that incredible woman."

"Woman?" my wife scoffed, "She was an angel sent to comfort you."

"I know she was," I said.

"Come on, dear," my wife told me, "it's time for the party!"

We do the work of angels when we reach out to someone.

Out of the Mouths of Babes

Alice had waited years to become a schoolteacher. She always joked that God had given her an ample lap so she could fill it with children. Not just any children, she knew in her heart, but children who perhaps didn't have a comfy or safe lap at home. Children who were scared about starting kindergarten. Children who simply wanted to sit close to an adult who wasn't talking on a cell phone, watching television, or quarreling.

Children had always been drawn to Alice like moths to the flame. It had seemed only natural that she enroll in education at the local college. It had been like coming home.

But so, too, had meeting the tall, sandy-haired young man who sat behind her in freshman English. She was a year short of graduation when they married and moved to a larger campus where her husband pursued his law degree.

Alice had willingly put her degree in early childhood education and her longed-for career on hold while she supported her husband in law school. She had worked in the college law library, keeping "her hand in" the life and career he had chosen. They had lunched together each day in the shadow of the statues outside the library. It was one of her favorite memories.

An attentive, caring husband, he had spent as much time with the family as he could, but he needed to work long hours to support their family while she stayed at home to raise their three children: two sons and a daughter. It was a mutual decision, and she never regretted postponing her second career.

Her whole family had all been in the front row the day, several years ago, when she had graduated from college, walking across the stage to receive her diploma.

Today, like the ladybug of nursery rhyme, her "...own children were all gone." They lived far away, and, when she had the time, it was fun to visit them. And although her house wasn't on fire, it could use a really good cleaning, as she was fond of saying. But a full-time kindergarten teacher didn't have enough hours in the day to bother with dusting, mopping, cleaning closets.

Alice smiled to herself at the thought. For it had been while digging in the back recesses of one of her son's closets that she had unearthed the first hat she took to school. If memory served, it had been a hat in the shape of a fish! She had worn it each day during "Science Time" while they were studying aquatic life.

It had become a trademark, Miss Alice's hats. Each hat brought with it some sort of lesson and connection to a bigger idea that Alice hoped the children would grasp.

There was the "Quiet Hat," actually a sleeping cap much like Scrooge in *The Christmas Carol* and the father in " 'Twas the Night Before Christmas" had worn. It signaled a need to come to the circle and sit quietly for a story or conversation. The children loved the "Thinking Hat"—an explorer's pith helmet, and they sometimes asked to be allowed to wear the

"Mad Hatter's Hat" when they were feeling cranky or out of sorts. The classroom rule was that when you saw someone wearing it, you offered a friendly smile but left them alone. And then there were hats for art, reading, math, recess, social studies, and every holiday.

Today, though, Alice would be showing them a hat she never thought she would have to bring into her bright classroom. Holding it in her lap, she surveyed the room with its lively, inviting bulletin boards, shelves of books, bug collections, aquarium, sand table, woodworking area.

She swallowed hard and called the children into a circle around her on the floor. Each child sat on a colored carpet square. They called this rug their "quilt," each square different and separate but connected. "Just like you," Miss Alice had explained.

"Today's hat is kind of an unusual hat you probably haven't seen very often." She held up a white turban of soft cotton and slipped it on her head.

"This is what I will look like for awhile. I have a sickness that means I won't be here with you for several weeks. You'll have a wonderful substitute teacher," she said, swallowing hard around the words. It was so difficult to relinquish these small souls to another's keeping.

Resolutely she continued. "The medicine that is going to make me better causes my hair to fall out, so I will be wearing this hat to keep my head warm. You know how it is at winter recess," she added.

The children nodded as if they understood the reasonableness of that. Alice was glad that she had decided to be frank with the children without alarming them. Facts bring freedom, she thought.

"I want each of you to sign my new hat," she continued, "so that each time I wear it I will think of you. And, of course, when I am thinking of you, you'll know it because that will be every time the sun comes up!" she said.

The children were uncharacteristically quiet during the rest of the day, and, without pushing or shoving, they took turns printing their names on the turban.

It was the first thing she packed for her stay in the hospital for surgery, the first step in her treatment.

The diagnosis had been grim, the outcome equally so. Everyone was hestitant to speak of it to Alice for fear of offering false hope, as some said, or making her cry.

Children waste no time in such evasions, and, when they took a field trip to the hospital to see her the day before she was released, they asked bluntly, "Are you going to be OK?"

"That's what we're planning,"Alice answered. "This is what's going to help me." She pointed to a bag of fluid hanging from an IV stand. It was her first chemotherapy treatment.

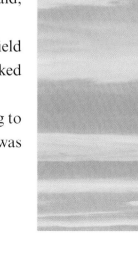

"Where's your hat?" the children asked.

She pointed to the signed turban draped jauntily on a water pitcher among the flowers and plants caring friends and family had brought. "I don't need it right now. Soon, though. And then I will come see you and model it," she said, making a promise she hoped she could keep.

"Bye, Miss Alice," they called, skipping away down the hall and back out to the big yellow school bus.

Alice sat at the window watching them and cried. Would she get to see them grow up? Help them learn to read? Begin to add numbers? Master all the words to the Pledge of Allegiance?

She felt her heart beginning to harden against loving those children so much. If she began distancing now, she thought slowly, perhaps it would not hurt so much . . . later. Perhaps it was best that they begin to forget about her now. She would discourage them from coming to see her again, she vowed.

Once home, she remained true to her vow. She could no longer afford the pain of being involved with children. She was always "too tired" to come to the phone when a child called or when several dropped by with their mothers to bring her cookies they had made. She let her husband take care of it. She put their letters and handmade cards and stories unread in a box and shoved it under her bed. She ignored an invitation to come to the school and let them read to her, for a change, on the class "quilt."

Children belonged in the past, along with hope.

Alice sat a little distance from the other patrons at the beauty shop. She was there getting her head shaved of what little hair was left from the cancer treatment begun in the hospital. When the stylist left to answer the phone at the front of the salon, a little boy appeared at Alice's knee.

Involuntarily she began to turn away.

"I hope you feel better," the little boy said solemnly. He handed her a white stuffed angel bear with quilted gold wings. "I will be thinking of you. All the children are. We love you."

She was touched more than the child could know. She was suffering from more than a disease...she had a bad case of the "lonelies," as she would've told her students.

Staring into the child's innocent, kind face, she felt her resolve at avoiding children begin to melt. It wasn't good to travel even this valley alone...for them as well as for me, she thought.

Perhaps I can stop by the school tomorrow and read to the children, if I feel well enough, she whispered to the stuffed bear. What a wonderful gesture, she thought, tucking it into her pocket. I must tell his mother what a kind child he is.

Later, when her hair was gone, her bald head gently washed and lotioned, Alice looked around for the child. He wasn't in sight; perhaps he was outdoors playing.

One by one, she checked with the other clients at the beauty shop to see whose child or grandchild he was so she could thank them for having such a mannerly child.

As one, they all looked at her as if the treatments had affected her mentally!

"There's not been a child here today!" the shop owner said, looking at her clients for confirmation. Alice knew better, putting her hand in her pocket and feeling the softness of the angel bear.

"I brought a friend with me," Alice tentatively told the oncology nurse on the first day of her outpatient treatments.

"Well, you bring him right along," the nurse said, leading the way into a bright, cheery room stenciled like an outdoor garden.

Together, they attached him to Alice's IV pole. Weekly, as she receives healing chemotherapy, angel bear smiles down at her. Each time she glances up at him, Alice knows that she is loved, supported, remembered, and accompanied by her own angel.

It's not your imagination. Sometimes a "coincidence" comes with a lot of angelic effort.

Look for the Silver Lining

I was having an especially stressful week. My family, my job, even the other people at church were pushing my nerves to the breaking point. I was getting ready to scream or cry, and I was not sure which it would be.

I was standing in my kitchen having my morning cup of coffee when, suddenly, from out of nowhere, I heard music. I wondered why the ice cream truck was coming so early in the morning. And then I realized the sound was coming from the top of my piano, where my music box collection was displayed. I raced into the living room and was amazed to see my mother's golden angel circling around. The melody "Look for the Silver Lining" rang joyously in my ears.

No train had rumbled by, no jets had passed overhead, no hand had touched the music box.

My mother had passed away ten years before, yet I knew she was still reaching out to me in some miraculous way, encouraging me to have a positive attitude about life.

The mechanism on my mother's angel, now my angel, had worn out ages ago and hadn't played for

several years. But that little music box sprang back to life that day—when I needed it most—uplifting my attitude and encouraging me to look for the best in whatever I encounter.

How grateful I am for that revitalizing melody. I have no doubt that my mother's tender spirit sent me those notes of joy.

Since that day, I have tried again and again to get the angel to play its sweet music, but to no avail. I guess if I really need to hear that song again, an angel will intervene.

Angels have appeared at every stage
in the evolution of humankind.
They've led the way of kings,
and they've witnessed miracles.
They've protected humanity
and run errands for God.

Angels on Earth

*I*n times of disaster or distress people sometimes encounter an angelic being. Often they see a heavenly "vision" or are helped by a kind soul who mysteriously disappears before being thanked. But angels come in many different forms, and Jack and Betty Vander Platt are living proof of that. Active volunteers since their teen years, Jack and Betty now go where the worst natural disasters strike, assisting the Red Cross in providing both physical and emotional assistance for those whose lives have been devastated. They truly are angels on earth.

As volunteers in the national Red Cross disaster response program, Jack and Betty respond to emergencies in their own region, nationally, and even overseas. Since their first Red Cross junket in 1993, they have faced hurricanes, wildfires, tornadoes, ice storms, earthquakes, and floods. They also serve in the volunteer fire department of their hometown, Wyckoff, in one of northern New Jersey's most scenic regions.

Following their basic training, Red Cross volunteers develop specialties through both experience and the many courses the disaster division makes available. Jack and Betty specialize in family assistance. Jack is a top coordinator, while Betty prefers to serve as a technician. On site, they work independently.

After initial overall damage assessment is done, service centers are set up where Jack's team analyzes each family's property to determine the kind of help they will require. Technicians such as Betty interview the families personally in an effort to ease their trauma and evaluate what it is they will need.

"Just imagine sitting across the table from one of us, being interviewed to assess your immediate emergency needs, and the only thing you have left for you and your family are the clothes on your back," says Jack. "They come to us completely devastated about it. Their hands shake. The kids hold on to their mother's skirts. You ask where the father is. He's standing by what—if anything—is left of the house to watch for looting of the little that may be left." Jack's voice falters; his eyes begin to water.

"You begin to talk with these people and help them to see a little light at the end of the tunnel...to realize there is a means of recovery, and we are there to help them get started. It's the most satisfying thing you can imagine, and we have tears in our eyes right along with them," he adds.

"I always like to say these experiences are a blessing for us," Betty chimes in. "We have been given the help and the strength to do these things. Money can't buy the gratification we get when we see a family who came in crying leave with smiles on their faces, hugging us and telling us how much they appreciate what we're doing for them."

One of the most harrowing assignments Jack has faced (Betty was unable to go with him) was the aftermath of Hurricane Georges, which cut a swath of destruction across the island of Puerto Rico in the fall of 1998. Any disaster scene is challenging for the volunteers who assist there, but this one seemed particularly so. When Jack stepped off the plane in Puerto Rico, he was immediately affected by the aftermath of Georges, the largest disaster the American Red Cross had ever been called on to handle. The airport terminal was dark. It was impossible to make a phone call. "So you stand there in a strange land where you can't speak the language. You discover a handful of other volunteers in the same situation. Finally some transportation comes, and they take you to your accommodations. Mine was a hotel in the little town of Catona, where I was to head up the service center for family relief."

When Jack registered at his hotel, the clerk handed him two candles, one for the bedroom and one for the bathroom. There was no power, so he had to walk up the four flights of stairs. Toilets could be flushed only once a day. The town water system had been destroyed, so the hotel brought in water in a former gasoline tank truck. The water was stored in a cistern and pumped to the roof by a small generator between 7 and 8 A.M. It then flowed by gravity to toilets and showers.

"I got wise and found a small waste can. I would store a little extra water in there so I could flush one more time," Jack laughs. "The room was unbelievably hot. I finally got an Allen wrench and figured out how to open the window. But that didn't do much good because the air outside was just as hot, and there was no breeze. It was almost impossible to sleep."

A freighter was brought into San Juan Bay with a million pounds of ice to protect formula for babies and drugs such as insulin that require refrigeration. In the heart of the towns and cities, debris was scattered everywhere, wires snaked across the ground, telephone poles were cracked, and branches were strewn all around. But the buildings still

stood—they are built of reinforced concrete. "When you got out of the center of the city, it was a very different story," Jack explains. Corrugated metal roofs were torn off. Walls were shattered. Metal louvers that served as windows were twisted out of shape.

"During the first days I was there, I did home visits. I'd go upstairs and be able to look up at the sky. The next day, I'd see one of the family members looking for assistance back in the service center, and they would tell me the house was now rain-protected and dry: The father had bent back the twisted metal roof and secured it with large nails."

While service centers are usually located in gymnasiums or similar structures, Jack's Catona team was forced to work out of a "mobile" center in a backyard under a tarpaulin to protect them from the sun. When it rained or the wind blew too hard, they moved to a woodworking shop that was severely damaged. "The chickens ran around our feet. The shop owner just sat and watched us because the damage made it impossible to work," Jack recalls.

The handful of stores that reopened in the early days following the hurricane were protected with metal fences. People clustered outside on the street. Inside, several clerks would take their orders and exchange merchandise and money through openings in the fence.

Jack's team in Catona included several locals who had previously qualified to do Red Cross disaster work. Many spoke English well enough to serve as translators. "That team of people was the most impressive I have ever worked with," Jack says. During his 23-day tour in Puerto Rico, Jack dispersed just short of $1 million in aid (in the form of vouchers) to 800 families.

"When disaster strikes and we need highly experienced volunteers, we always turn to the Vander Platts," says Kimberly Saul, director of emergency services for the Bergen Crossroads chapter of the Red Cross. "Betty and Jack are nationally respected for their work on disasters. We are particularly fortunate to have them in our area for local emergencies. Their knowledge and ability to implement that knowledge is a key component of our successful disaster relief locally."

The Vander Platt home is in a constant state of readiness. In an office lined with disaster-response manuals, a computer for checking weather (providing tip-offs of impending disasters) shares space with Betty's sewing machine. When Hurricane Georges struck, Jack was called at noon and asked whether he could go. At 6 P.M. he was called again and told to move fast. At 71 years old, Jack has turned over most of his business duties to his sons, so he has the freedom to respond almost instantly. He and his wife like to be prepared for whenever they might be called to action.

Jack and Betty know their services are needed, and they gain a lot of satisfaction from the help they are able to provide. However, they recently passed on one assignment without regret. With almost 100 invitations sent out and a gala party scheduled, the Vander Platts stayed home last year to celebrate their fiftieth wedding anniversary. As much as they enjoy helping others, sometimes even angels need to put their family first.

Guiding Angels

Angels find us, not only

when we need them most,

but even when we think we are

fine on our own.

The Voice

Somehow my grandparents, who were raising me, and I managed to survive the ravages of World War II in our native Hungary. But when that terrible war finally ended in 1945, no jubilation arose because Soviet troops immediately held our country hostage in the arms of communism. Suddenly, people who spoke out against the new oppressions taking place were rounded up by the recently formed secret police force and never seen again.

My grandfather, a retired judge, continued to speak out, and, in the fall of 1945, two men appeared at our house to take him away. They said he was being taken in for questioning only. Grandfather, pointing out that his hands were dirty from working in the garden, asked if he could wash up first. The men agreed. When he didn't come out of the bathroom right away, the men ran and pushed the door open. The water in the sink was still running, but Grandfather was gone. He had jumped out the bathroom window and fled on foot.

After Grandfather went into hiding, life became even more difficult for Grandmother and me. We lived on soup made from the potatoes and other vegetables grown in our garden, and we never knew when the secret police would show up again to search our house. Sometimes they came in the middle of the night, breaking down the door in hopes of finding Grandfather. Fear became our constant companion and prayer our sustenance.

For two years my grandfather managed to elude capture, and, although he sent word to us of his safety, most of the time we did not know his whereabouts. Grandmother and I missed him terribly. The thought that we might never be together again plagued me constantly. But on an autumn day in 1947, when I was ten years old, it seemed as though the time had come for us to be reunited.

When new elections were held in our country, I waited for the results with great interest. The next morning our radio announced that the communist party had been defeated. Celebrations erupted in the streets, with none of us realizing that the communist government, backed by Soviet troops, wasn't about to give up that easily, elections or no elections.

Certainly, after listening to the radio broadcast, my ten-year-old mind concluded that the election results meant that Grandfather could come home and we could be a family again. I wondered if Grandfather, who we recently learned was hiding out on a nearby farm, had heard the good news. I decided now was the time to hike to the farm and tell him. Then we could come home together and surprise Grandma! Of course, I didn't tell anyone of my plan. Rather than go to school, I set out on the long walk out of town to Grandfather's hiding place. As I reached the outskirts of our village without having drawn any attention to myself, wild anticipation filled my heart. In a short while I would see Grandfather for the first

time in two years, and we would walk home together and live as a family again. My eyes filled with tears of joy, and I began to walk faster.

Suddenly I was startled when I heard a man's voice call my name. I stopped dead in my tracks and looked all around, but I saw no one. "Who are you? Where are you?" I asked quietly, straining to see if he might be hiding in some nearby bushes.

"It isn't important where I am," the voice replied. "I am here to warn you that you are putting your grandfather in grave danger, for you are being followed. Turn around and go back to your grandmother immediately, and know that you will all be together again soon."

Frightened now, I immediately turned and began running back toward the village. My heart was pounding so hard I thought it would jump right out of my chest. I ran past a man on a bicycle and recognized him as one of the secret police. The stranger's voice had been right: I was being followed!

When I reached our house, I found Grandma outside pacing back and forth in the street. "Oh, thank God you are all right!" she cried, gathering me in her arms. "They came to tell me that you were not in school, and I thought someone had taken you away."

"I decided to go and tell Grandfather that the communists lost the election," I wailed. "I thought we could come home together and surprise you!"

"Oh, my!" Grandma said, shaking her head in disbelief.

"But someone stopped me," I continued. "A voice told me I was being followed and that I should go back home. It was the kindest, most loving

voice I have ever heard, Grandma. I believe it was the voice of God speaking to me. No one else knew of my plan. No one!"

My grandmother nodded silently, ushered me into the house, and continued to hold me for a long time. Then she reassured me that everything would be better soon.

Two weeks later, a man came to get us in the middle of the night. By the time the sun rose, we had traveled many miles to a place near the Austrian border where a large group of ethnic Germans were about to be deported into Austria. My heart leapt when I saw Grandfather there. He looked lovingly into my eyes and hugged me tight. We were to be smuggled out of our country as ethnic Germans. Recognizing the danger still around us, we didn't dare breathe a sigh of relief until we crossed into Austria. There, we ended up in a refugee camp along with hundreds of other destitute refugees, but at least we were finally together again.

Grandfather remained fearful that the long arm of communism could still reach out and snatch him back. It wasn't until 1951, when we were given a chance at new lives in our wonderful new country, the United States of America, that he was finally able to relax and live out his life in peace.

Over the years, I have often wondered about the voice I heard on that fall day in 1947. I speculated that the voice might have belonged to some kind neighbor who had guessed my destination and decided to warn me anonymously. Or perhaps it really was the voice of an angel that prompted me to turn around. Whether the voice was human or heavenly, I know one thing for sure: God's hand guided us safely back together so we could be a family again.

On the Job

"*L*ife is not a dress rehearsal."

Ellie had heard herself say these words dozens, probably hundreds of times. And who could count the instances when she had heard it growing up? The saying, like her straight dark hair now beginning to show more than a few threads of gray, slightly upturned nose, and the recipe for good crab cakes (always served with buttery corn on the cob and fresh blueberry muffins), was handed down to her by her grandmother like family silver.

Grandmother, or Grandmom as her 11 grandchildren had lovingly called her, had been a violin player in the prestigious university symphony orchestra. She had often performed in the orchestra pit accompanying a production put on by the university's opera department. Grandmom knew the difference between "live performances" and "dress rehearsals."

"What would Grandmom think of me now?" Ellie wondered as she dried her hair one morning before work. Grandmom had raised her, teaching Ellie independence, resiliency, joy in living, and a sense of adventure. Grandmom had also been Ellie's biggest cheerleader and coach when she tried something new.

Ellie wished that her grandmother were around to help her decide what to do, but Grandmom had been gone, her music silenced, for several years. In addition to the similarities in their appearance that kept Ellie and Grandmom connected, there was also lavender.

Ellie closed her eyes. She could smell the faint aroma that always preceded Grandmom when she entered a room. And, even though she knew it wasn't possible to smell fragrance from such a distance, Ellie, as a child in the audience, always believed that she could smell the lavender-scented handkerchief Grandmom tucked beneath her chin while she played the violin. Ellie kept a pot of fresh lavender on her windowsill year-round, and her sidewalks were lined with the waving purple-tipped flowers.

If I keep up the way I'm going, Ellie thought wryly as she locked the house behind her, the decision isn't going to be up to me: I will be fired and can stay home and putter in the flowers from dawn to dusk! Each day she was getting to work later and later.

The social service agency where she was supervisor of caseworkers providing home healthcare and other supportive services for senior citizens had recently been "adopted" by another, larger governmental department. Changes in her department, where she had worked for nearly 20 years, were draining the joy from a vocation she loved despite its relentless pace, pressing needs, often depressing situations, and so-so salary. But for each elderly person she helped stay independent and safe and secure, she felt like she was taking care of Grandmom.

The final straw, however, came when the new management moved Ellie's desk into a windowless, soundproof, professional-looking, and super-efficient cubicle. It was, in Ellie's opinion, little more than a file drawer for people. She stood on her desk chair and looked up and down the rows of similar cubicles—or drawers—and felt that she was slowly shrinking to the point of becoming invisible.

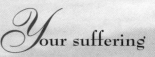

Your suffering may make an angel weep into her wings, but it will never make her walk away.

Isolation, to management thinking as they explained when challenged, would improve productivity, cut down on interoffice chatter, and boost output of cases. This about employees who were by their very nature and career choice gregarious, people-oriented, chatty, and workaholics!

Ellie was spokesperson for a group of employees who asked for compromise about removing some of the cubicle walls.

"We need to talk to one another about cases we share," she explained, holding up charts and files.

Management was adamant, holding up their charts pointing to already improved efficiency and speedier delivery of services.

As if, thought Ellie, dealing with other people's lives the way she and her fellow caseworkers did could be measured on a calculator and weighed like so much fish on a scale.

Ellie didn't know which was worse, not being able to look out a window to the maple tree across the street or not being able to talk with her coworkers. They had shared daily chitchat for years…chitchat about one another's lives, children, joys. And, most importantly, about their cases.

"My job," Ellie heard herself say aloud one day in her little file drawer of an office, "is also not a dress rehearsal."

Knowing this to be true made it easier, then, when it came time to make a decision about staying or leaving the department. Ellie only struggled a few months before submitting her resignation.

Her heart was heavy, her mind numb from sleepless nights wrestling with uneasy feelings that she was being a quitter. Others were sticking it out, but she just couldn't do it any longer.

"After all," she told coworkers, family, and friends, "life is not a dress rehearsal."

But when was the "real" event she wondered as she packed the accumulation of stuff from her desk and removed pictures from the cubicle's walls. When was the "full, live" performance to be? She was nearing 50 years old, and roles for middle-aged women were few and far between.

It was a question she pondered with increasing frequency as days became months. She was restless and filled her time doing jobs for a temporary placement agency. She answered phones for a dentist, filed briefs for a law firm, typed letters for a bank vice president, and stayed a year at a business that managed shopping malls all over the world. Despite the fact that she got a trip to London out of that one, it, like all the other jobs, had the pinching feel of wearing a shoe that doesn't quite fit.

She began volunteering. She served on many committees, puttered in the garden, and cleaned house until she couldn't stand her own reflection in the polished mirrors and sparkling windows.

Although Ellie hadn't been around children since she'd been one and much preferred working with the elderly, she jumped at the chance to fill in for a friend who was scheduled to read to children at the local hospital.

She was nervous and chose her books carefully after consulting with a librarian, two friends who were grandmothers, and a school teacher. Ellie even wrote out a little introduction and had a few jokes and tricks up her sleeve, including tying knots in one of Grandmom's hankies to make a baby in a cradle.

On reading day, she spoke in different voices for each book character. The children gathered around her chair in the pediatric department lobby. Some were in wheelchairs, some in wagons tethered to IV poles, some on crutches, and still others on parents' or nurses' laps. The kids hung on every word as Ellie read, gasping in surprise or clapping their hands in delight as the "characters" acted out their parts as Ellie portrayed them.

It was an entirely unexpected reunion.

Ellie loved the patients, they loved her. It felt like coming home. The parents of these very ill small-fry patients clustered around her at the end of the reading session asking when she would be coming back. Many parents said it was the first time their child had laughed or showed some of their old spark. As they talked, they unburdened themselves to Ellie, much as families of her elderly clients had done.

"Oh, this was just a one-time gig," Ellie said lightly, as she packed up her books and tricks.

Angels can be pushy. For your own good, of course. They know the words in your heart and help you get them out thought Ellie as she sat waiting in her car in the parking lot at the hospital a month after she had first read to the children. She had driven back today to pick up library books she'd left behind in her haste to get out of there—fast! Ellie had no intention of staying or getting involved in conversation. Dash in, get the books, dash home.

Now she checked her appearance in the rearview mirror. She still looked the same. But inside she felt different. Whole, satisfied, but still surprised.

Not an hour before, she'd seen her words, as in a cartoon balloon, float from her mouth as she applied for a job.

"Do you think there would ever be a part-time job as a support person in your department?" Ellie had questioned. "My credentials are in the geriatric-support field, but it's not that great a distance to these little guys."

Ellie didn't know who had been more astounded, her or the supervising nurse. It had been as if someone was off-stage prompting Ellie from a script that she'd not had the courage to write herself.

"Let's go to my office before you change your mind," the nurse manager had said, holding Ellie's elbow lest she change her mind.

Ellie started the car. She sniffed the air. It carried on it the faint fragrance of lavender. And then she knew. An angel with a lavender-laced handkerchief tucked up her sleeve, out of sight in the orchestra pit, was nudging her to move on, move out, move toward who God was calling her to be in the fullest performance of her life.

Lessons From a Guiding Angel

Every time I pass a playground full of children, I see the faces of angels laughing and playing.

oint, click. With a little searching on my computer, I found confirmation of my feelings. I reread the computer screen: "No little girl dreams of growing up and becoming a stepmother."

No truer words were likely spoken, but here I, at 34 years old, had become one. Two lively boys, John, 10, and Thomas, 8, had come to live with their father, Jay, and me. Needless to say, weekends and spring break visits hadn't been adequate preparation.

The first week was particularly difficult for me. After two years of quiet life as a couple, I was thrust into hectic family living. It was a major transition, since I had no children of my own. On top of this, I was adjusting to life in a large townhouse complex, which we had moved into a month earlier.

"Dear God," I prayed, "who am I?"

I knew I couldn't replace the boys' mom, and not enough time had passed for me to be seen as a trusted friend. So I took the only role I saw open to me: a quiet worker in the shadows.

In the days and weeks after the boys arrived, I located after-school programs, set up doctor's appointments, filled out countless forms, bought the boys' favorite foods, and did mounds and mounds of laundry. . . in the shadows. Each night before bed, I watched the children hug their father and say, "I love you." I wondered how long it would take for me to receive even an acknowledgment, much less appreciation or affection. Although the boys didn't resent me—they were glad I was in their lives and in their father's, too—it was discouraging to admit they might never see me as more than an outsider.

As I searched the Internet for information about my new role, I became even more discouraged. Web sites discussed both pros and cons of being a stepmother, but I was so frightened I only focused on the cons. What I read validated how I felt: Many women said being a stepmother was a thankless job and the most challenging thing they had ever done. Others talked of having a strained relationship with their stepchildren and wanting life to be easier.

In my worry and fear, I turned to God, continuing to ask, "Who am I? What is my role with these children? Why am I here?"

Conversations with God were still somewhat new for me, a former nonpracticing believer. But four years ago, without hesitation, as if welcoming me home, God had reached out and taken me in. Now I was grateful to be able to lift my concerns to him in prayer.

I had always been aware that God loved, guided, and accepted me, but my full change of heart and desire to have a personal relationship with him happened during a public television show about angels. At first I was skeptical, but I was also intrigued. Curious, I tried some of the suggestions on the show about how to look and listen for your angels. A whole new world opened up to me as I became aware of the gentle thoughts, images, words, and answers that were available to me. I was no longer alone. Not that I had been—I was just unaware of how surrounded by love I actually was. Since that day, I have never looked back.

Now, with a calm certainty that God and his angels were also in this new family relationship with me, I waited to see how the Lord was going to use me—and help me, for I had no doubt that he would. Since my acceptance of him and my own guardian angels, I had felt the presence of a guiding hand. Surely I would not be left alone now. Again I prayed, "Who am I?"

A feeling of great comfort swept over me as God's answer came swiftly, "You are their guiding angel."

Why, of course! I thought. God's angels are beside us each day, although we are often too busy, too afraid, or too uninformed to realize this. Angels, too, perform endless acts of love and assistance without receiving much acknowledgment. Or do they? I wondered. Do I?

Of course, I realized with joy, we all receive acknowledgment in the form of God's love and guidance and his daily gifts of beauty in the world.

As I continued to pray and meditate, I also realized that instead of the children thanking me, God was saying "thank you" for them. His "thanks" come in many forms: the sun on my face, a silky orange flower, a cheerful neighbor, a beautiful sunset, the feeling of his hand on my shoulder. If I continued to look for thanks from the children, I could be disappointed. But if I looked for my thanks from God, I would never be let down.

Even so, I struggled to understand, praying, "Why me? Why am I with these children?"

Again, the answer came swiftly: "To learn, to love, and to help yourself." I realized that God had a question for me: What are you going to make from this?

Perhaps I'll help make a family, I thought. Perhaps we can find unity instead of just being four individuals.

In the process, I have learned from watching the unconditional love that flows between the boys and their father. I've also learned that a little love can go a long way. One night, I was alone with one of the boys. Quietly, I talked to him about "boy topics" such as bugs, fishing, and video games. While I did not verbally express my loving feelings to him, I looked at him with warmth and with interest. He was relaxed and comfortable, and he seemed to genuinely enjoy my company. I know I enjoyed his. I was that loving presence beside him that night. I was his guiding angel. I'm excited to play this role in his life.

Angels, I believe, can't shield us from our consequences, so I am learning not to interfere with the boys and their father when they are having trouble. Instead, I help them understand, profit from the experience, and reach out again. Learning to deal with disappointment is a part of life, and it makes us stronger. I cannot stand in the way of the boys' development. I can only let God lead the way.

Actually, I prefer to have God lead, for it isn't a job I do comfortably. My requests to turn off the television or stay in the house, for instance, are usually met with rolling eyes and unhappy faces. I've had to learn that my

need to be liked interferes with being a confident leader. I have to love, appreciate, and trust myself; I can't expect to receive the children's constant approval. As mothers know, it doesn't always come!

As I recognize my thank-yous from God, I also look to him for the love I want. It's natural for the children to be hesitant with me, and, even

as I yearn for their affection, I know I must remain patient. The boys are slowly beginning to show me "little loves," like sharing confidences, a few quick smiles, and even—occasionally—brief thank-yous.

I've also discovered that this new family routine is helping me to become more productive. I get up early each day and accomplish a lot. I'm a better time manager now, and I have goals I'm actively pursuing instead of just thinking about them. Accepting my role as their angel, I'm motivated to be the best caretaker I can be, for my husband, the boys, and myself.

The recent holidays were good for our family, for that is what we are becoming. After just a few months, the boys have started to seek me out. They are beginning to trust what I have to offer—and I am, too. I've found many opportunities to help them with self-esteem and motivation. I've gained patience and insight about discovering what they need and then helping to provide it. I'm also helping them learn the value of dealing with

tough times. A new school, of course, provides a daily opportunity for such lessons. I help them look at rough spots and say, "Hmm, now, how can I make this different?" or "Next time, I'll respond this way when such-and-such happens." Each and every day is a new learning experience for all of us.

I am comforted by God's answer about who I am, for now my identity crisis is solved, and my purpose is clear. Choosing to learn, love, and help myself has changed my perspective from the frightened, powerless person I was when I first read that computer message. I've begun looking for a support group of stepmothers who share their concerns and, yes, even the joys of being in such a unique relationship with children and God . . . the perfect spot for a guiding angel.

When you feel lost, pause and look closely around you. Somewhere, somehow, an angel will be waiting to guide you home.

Turn-About's Fair Play

*I*f it hadn't been for Frances, I probably would have been a juvenile delinquent. Or worse: an adult delinquent.

I was on my way, today, to a reunion of sorts. I had albums and scrapbooks filled with articles about my growing career as a playwright at the back of the book. The front pages, however, contained pictures and stories from my time with Frances, the person who gave me direction in my life when I needed it.

Our family was new in town that summer. I was the middle son, with a younger brother and sister, and an older, bossy sister. None of us had wanted to move from the small town where we were born and where our parents had been teachers at the local high school.

After years of night school, however, Dad had earned his degree in educational administration. In short, now he could be a principal. If there is anything worse than having parents for teachers in the school you attend, it's having a father as principal. You know, the guy who patrols the hallways, stalking the tardy, the unruly. Or, as we kids tried to point out, the innocent.

School was starting in less than a month when we arrived in the upscale suburban community that had hired my father. The high school was a monstrous affair of glass, attached buildings, and the state football champions. Since I was a bespectacled, bookworm type of kid, I was not impressed. But, then, neither were the few kids I'd met all that impressed with me.

Teen years are hard enough with people you've known all your life. With strangers, it's pretty grim. I had discovered, however, that truancy, shoplifting, and small mischief earned you notoriety of sorts. I wasn't sure which group of kids I'd be included in: geek or gang member.

One Saturday morning, I was hanging around some of the tougher guys shooting basketball in the yard next door to my house. I'd had my hands on the basketball only twice all morning. But, at least, I'd consoled myself, I hadn't broken any laws and nobody had beat me up.

Yet.

I looked up—my fate as a geek was about to be sealed. Here came our elderly neighbor, Frances.

She lived across the street in a small brick house with a yard of flowers, carefully edged lawn, and an antique red Pontiac convertible her late husband had restored. Frances drove it everywhere. I secretly admired it but avoided getting too close in case Frances saw me looking at it and wanted to talk. But here she came, looking for all the world like she was coming to talk to me. I had met her the day we moved in; she had brought over supper for us. My parents immediately fell in love with her.

She couldn't have been five feet tall, and she walked with the rapid gait of a bird chasing seed. Her white hair was dyed an amazing shade of pale blue, and her clothes ran mostly to long-sleeved, ankle-length flowery dresses buttoned to the neck even in the summer heat.

My heart sank as she came closer. I looked around in hope that she was coming over to see my mother or father. But no, she marched straight up to me.

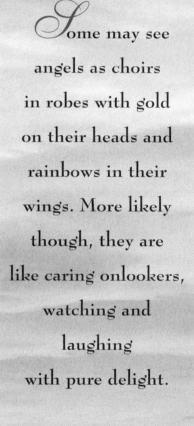

Some may see angels as choirs in robes with gold on their heads and rainbows in their wings. More likely though, they are like caring onlookers, watching and laughing with pure delight.

The guys behind me kept playing basketball but paused long enough to nod greetings, mumbling, "Hello, Miss Frances."

She acknowledged them with a friendly wave then pulled me aside.

"I would like you to come over tonight and meet some people," she said.

When I hesitated, she fixed me with a surprisingly piercing gaze that held just a hint of laughter. "I already cleared it with your parents," she said innocently.

I was done for.

I promised to mow the lawn, wash the car, walk the dog, carry out the garbage, and even tutor my youngest sister in math for the rest of our natural lives if my parents would not make me go over to Frances's house.

They stood firm, not caring that a simple trip across the street was about to change my life forever.

Or, maybe, as I've had occasion to wonder since then, they did know what the outcome would be.

At any rate, when I arrived, I encountered an unlikely group of friends that boasted this elderly lady as its center.

Fragile as a violet in a flowing purple dress, she was surrounded by teenagers in assorted shapes, styles, and moods. There were geeks like me, but there were also kids with colored hair, pierced body parts, too much makeup, and even one roundly pregnant girl who couldn't have been a day over 14.

"I'd like you to meet my new friend," Frances said, pulling me toward her. "I think he has interesting plays to share with us. Perhaps we can each read a part to help him see how they'll work onstage."

I looked at her, my mouth open: My writing was a secret.

No one, not my parents, siblings, or best friend back home, knew that I spent hours creating fictional worlds where I laid out characters' lives in acts, scenes, costumes. I was going to be a playwright.

Frances, as I discovered, wasn't just any old lady, she was best friend to teens who met once a week at her house to do homework, play cards—she was teaching them bridge—but mostly to talk. Nothing shocked her, and nothing surprised her. Eventually we all simply gave up trying and enjoyed her friendship.

She taught us to hold a spoon properly, and we read aloud from the classics…and, in time, from our own writings. The first person ever to act in one of my musicals was Frances. I will always hear her voice projecting the very emotion I'd hoped for. Not even seeing my plays turned into movies or winning prestigious awards will ever equal seeing Frances lead the cast of that mismatched group of kids saying and singing my words.

A messenger of love, she gently drew it from us, too, guiding us to become the people she knew we could be. Strangely, though, she always insisted we were the angels God sent to her…keeping her alert, vigorous, she said, "…and young at heart."

Today I read from my newest play for Frances. It was the least I could do. For today was her funeral at the church she loved. And, as we say in my business, "…we were playing to a full house."

247

People had come to let the curtain fall on this earthly chapter of an inspired, inspiring life. I took my place in front of an impromptu choir formed of many of the young people who'd gathered at Frances's house all those years ago. Most of us were well into our thirties and forties now. We were having a reunion after the service. I looked forward to seeing where Miss Frances's messages of love had taken these long-ago friends.

I raised my hand, ready to give the downbeat in front of the choir, and I felt I was once again in Frances's living room.

Stand straight, she whispered in my ear.

And then we began to sing. The melody was simple so no rehearsal had been necessary—it was our final good-bye to Miss Frances. As if inspired, our voices rose in sweetest song, echoing the truth that friendship knows no age barriers. Surprisingly, in that truth, perhaps we did sound just a little bit like an angel chorus singing for one of our own.

I will always believe that it wasn't a trick of lighting that drew my eye upward that day. There Frances was, watching, nodding, and humming in eager support as she always had. Sunlight was glinting off her old gold spectacles, their radiance reflecting in the stained glass splendor.

Get out of the Rough

Matt warmed up with a few practice swings. It would be fun to play a round with his old high school teammates even though the occasion wasn't a happy one. It was appropriate though, Matt thought. Coach Hunter would have loved the idea of his old golfers getting together for a tournament after his memorial service.

Matt wished his old coach were there with them so he could tell him about his new job. He was making more money than he'd ever dreamed possible. Who'd have thought he'd be making nearly $100,000 just one year out of college. Matt's buddies were mighty impressed when he told them in response to their questions.

"I thought only gangsters pulled in that kind of dough," teased Brian.

"Or pro golfers," called Andy. "And you'll never be a professional."

Matt laughed. "Seems to me I made more money playing golf than any of you guys did. I was always the one who won the quarters when we bet on who'd be closest to the pin."

When it was Matt's turn to tee off, he had a clean hit right down the middle of the fairway. A little short, but a good drive.

"Coach Hunter would have called us wimps if he'd caught us riding in this cart," said Brian as they bounced along the path toward their balls.

"He was a great man," said Matt. "He taught us as much about life as he taught us about golf." Both men were silent for a few moments thinking of the impact their mentor had on their lives.

To change the subject, Brian said, "So tell me about this high-paying dream job of yours."

"There's lots of good things about the job beside the money," said Matt.

He went on to explain that selling computer software to health and fitness centers was perfect for him because it combined his love of sports with his interest in computers. "But," he said as he pulled the cart to a stop for Brian to hit. "There are some aspects about the job I don't much like."

Matt and Brian didn't have a chance to get back to their conversation until the long fifth hole. "So what is it about the job you don't like," asked Brian.

Matt frowned. "I don't think my company's any worse than most others, but it is sometimes hard to feel good about promising that software will arrive on a specific date and then not have it be there on time."

"That's probably the nature of the business," said Brian. He drove the cart into shade while they waited for the group ahead of them to putt in.

"It bothers me, too," said Matt, "that my bosses want me to tell customers that our new products will be compatible with their old computers. They may work, but they don't always work together very well."

Brian reached behind his seat for his water bottle. "Got to stay hydrated you know." He looked down the fairway. "Looks like the green is clear. You're away. Go for it."

Matt climbed out of the cart. He reached into his bag, pulled out his three iron, and walked over to his ball. Remembering to keep his head down and his hands firm, he got off a long, long drive.

He and Brian shielded their eyes to follow its flight path right toward the rough. "I must have forgotten to focus on the direction I wanted the ball to travel."

"Guess we're all a little rusty," said Brian. "If you think you can find it, Andy and Kevin and I will hit."

"I'm pretty sure it's in the tall grass just beyond that second lodgepole pine. I'll flag you guys down if I don't locate it right away."

As Matt walked along the edge of the fairway, he thought of another aspect of his job that bothered him. Just a couple of days earlier he'd learned how hard it was for his customers to cash in on the rebate he'd promised them. He'd rationalized that hardly any customers bothered to cash in on rebates anyway, but his discovery still made him uncomfortable.

The white object Matt had been walking toward turned out to be a duck feather rather than his ball. He carefully searched the ground in front

of the pine. There it was! His ball was sitting just on the edge of the rough but touching an out-of-bounds line.

Matt remembered a time five years earlier when he'd been in a similar spot. "Don't forget to count that as a penalty stroke," Coach Hunter had called out to him. Matt could hear his words as clearly now as if his

old coach were standing there beside him. "If you're not in bounds, you're out of bounds." Matt understood the message. He realized why he'd received it. If you're not honest, you are dishonest . . . in life just as in golf.

Straddling the ball, he swung. The ball lofted out onto the fairway, not far from where his friends' balls rested. Matt hurried to where the other golfers were waiting.

"Your ball must have landed in a lucky spot," said Andy.

"You're right about that," said Matt. "I'll need to take a penalty stroke for being out-of-bounds, but I'm going to follow Coach Hunter's advice and focus on the direction I want to travel through life."

He got out his nine iron and chipped up onto the green. As soon as I get back home, he promised himself, I'm going to begin looking for a job where I can play by the rules all the time.

To hope is to fly. To fly is to dream. To dream is to believe.
To believe is to do. To do is to give hope. To give hope
is to fight the fight of angels.

Loving Angels

When you live with a heart of

compassion, you have the heart of an angel.

When you fill your life with deeds of

compassion, you do the work

of an angel.

On Elephants and Angels

My grandmother held that all of us, at least once in our lifetime, would encounter an angel in disguise. Mine came in the being of a 19-year-old mentally challenged woman dressed in a hospital housekeeper's uniform. Her name was Angie.

I was 22 when I meet Angie. Seemingly healthy other than some swelling and a few pesky sores on my legs, I was hospitalized for tests. It took four months for them to diagnose an inflammation of my blood vessels caused by systemic lupus. This caused severe leg problems. My right leg was amputated, and I was left with nerve damage and deformity of my left leg and foot. Worse yet, as far as my vanity was concerned, I ballooned from a size 9 to a size 22 from massive steroid intake. The steroids also distorted my facial features and body shape. The crowning blow was the loss of my hair from aggressive chemotherapy. I'd stopped looking in the mirror to avoid gawking at the bald, bloated creature that stared back.

Only Angie seemed oblivious to the ravages of my illness. Every other visitor averted their eyes. Even nurses seemed to look anywhere but at me. My boyfriend, Mike, came less and less, finally fading away altogether. In my worst moments, I imagined God turning away also.

But Angie! My angel. The clinking of her massive key ring announced her arrival each morning. I found myself looking forward to her somewhat awkward attempts to mop my floor. The huge industrial mop proved

too cumbersome for her jerky, hesitant body movements. But what she lacked in cleaning ability, Angie made up for with her charm.

"Hi," she greeted me daily. She'd walk straight to my bed and look directly at me with her huge brown eyes. "Are you better today?"

She asked with such utter sincerity and hope that I felt obligated to answer "a little better," even on my worst days. Angie would then grin and set about her tasks. While she worked, she shared stories about her mom, her sister, Lucy, and her pet cat, Boo. And sometimes she shared a prayer. Before leaving the room, she never failed to ask if I needed anything.

One morning, during Angie's regular visiting time, I was on a stretcher in the hallway waiting for a ride to the operating room for a bone graft. I'd lost count of the number of such trips I had made in the past few months as surgeons struggled to save my remaining leg. I felt despondent and full of self-pity. God seemed farther away than ever.

A tear trickled down my cheek. As I turned toward the wall to wipe the tear away, I felt a tap on my shoulder. There stood Angie, her face full of love and concern. She pressed something into my hand.

"You hold it," she said. "It always gives me the best luck."

She had placed a blue plastic elephant in my hand; it had always hung on her key ring.

"I won it at the fair," she said. "It's blue, just like your eyes."

I smiled. Through all my ailments and deformities, Angie saw the one part of me that had not changed—my eyes. She loved me the way God did—unconditionally. My spirits soared.

"Thanks, Angie," I said. "I'll take good care of it."

The blue elephant saw me through the surgery, then months of physical therapy and rehabilitation in a different hospital building. The grueling job of learning to live again took most of my time, but I found myself missing Angie. Once in a while, she would stop by my new room on her way home and visit for a few minutes before she had to leave to catch her bus. She always had a funny story about Boo's latest feline escapades. Those were my best days.

When the morning of my discharge finally arrived, Angie was right there. She insisted I keep the elephant. "So you'll remember me," she added.

I gave her a big hug. "I'll always remember you, Angie."

She grinned. "You're my friend. I'll remember you, too."

Over the next few years, I sent notes and cards to Angie through the housekeeping department of the hospital. Then one day my letter was returned. Angie no longer worked there. She had moved with her family and left no forwarding address. But I still have contact with Angie through the little blue elephant that sits on my mantel.

No other gift will ever compare to this treasured gift of unconditional love from an angel in disguise.

When we are in touch with the angels, we walk to a heavenly rhythm that guides our way.

Nicholas

My son Nicholas has always had a soft heart. It's the thing I love best about him. At 13, he is now struggling with the "macho" role society expects of him despite having a tender heart that still wants to save every homeless person and rescue each stray kitten. I am proud that he has remained a compassionate and kind person, even though the teenage years have struck. One of my proudest moments was when he decided to give Christmas to a family in our neighborhood.

Chad and Derek Williams are two boys who attend Nick's junior high. Junior high is painful enough for anyone, but for Chad and Derek it is a daily nightmare. They live alone with their mother, and they are the smallest boys in junior high. The boys are picked on constantly, partly because they wear the same worn, outdated clothes to school every day. Their mother is a loving, hardworking woman, but she is a single mom and there is rarely enough money left over for clothes.

My son has always been sensitive to the pain of others. While most teenage kids wouldn't have even noticed, Nick immediately understood their embarrassment. They quickly became the subject of Nick's prayers and worries. He appointed himself secret protector to Chad and Derek.

Every year at Christmas our family selects a family and becomes their "Secret Santa." Last Christmas we had a family meeting to select a family. Everyone voted, and the majority of our family voted for a disabled

friend of ours, who also happened to be a single mom with two teenagers. Nicholas voted for Chad and Derek's family. I could see the determination and concern in his blue-gray eyes. We discussed the needs of each family. Again we voted. Again, the majority vote went to the other family. But my son resolutely stuck to his decision to help the Williams boys. Not wanting to squelch my son's desire to make a difference in other peoples' lives, I hesitated. I knew how important this family was to him. I also thought we couldn't afford to provide for two families. My husband and I had a short conference, and we made a decision.

We would be Secret Santas for both families. Nicholas's eyes lit up. The grin on his 13-year-old face made my heart soar. How many mothers are blessed with a teenage angel? Seeing the kindness in my child's soul brought tears to my eyes. I knew what a rarity he was, and I would do everything within my power to see that his Christmas wish was fulfilled.

It is our tradition to provide the makings of a Christmas dinner, as well as to give carefully selected gifts for the family. Nick wanted to buy the boys clothes—but not just any clothes. They had to be "cool"; they had to be "in" clothes. At my ripe old age of 34, I was not qualified to know what was "in." Nick was determined to give Chad and Derek clothes that would stop the taunting and make them feel good about what they wore to school. To many of us, this may be trivial, but to a young teenager, it is everything. Whether he realized it or not, Nick wanted to give them self-esteem, a chance to fit in. That's quite a gift for a 13-year-old to give.

As we spent endless hours looking for just the right outfits for the boys, I reflected on their mother. I knew a little about what she must be feeling and sacrificing. I remembered the days of my own single motherhood, when every little "extra" went to my children's needs. It had probably been a long time since she had done anything nice for herself. Abandoning the kids to the boys' clothing department, I took a quick detour to the bath aisle. Smiling to myself, I selected a bath basket, filled to the brim with bubbles, soaps, lotions, and all kinds of "take me away" things that only a mom can appreciate. I found myself catching Nicholas's spirit. Not knowing the boys' mother well, I searched the store for other gifts that would give her a lift. I looked at clothes, makeup, jewelry, books. I finally selected a book of uplifting stories for moms and a box of truffles. Delighted with myself, I couldn't wait to show everyone. The spirit of Christmas filled my heart and overflowed into a joyous, childlike feeling of giddiness.

Returning to my children, I found they had finally settled on several articles of clothing that my son thought were "in." Judging the boys' sizes was difficult, but we did our best. Nick suddenly remembered the boys wore only old, worn coats to school. And Utah winters demanded good, warm gloves. We chose the thickest, warmest, "coolest" gloves in the store, and I didn't even look at the price tag! We were all grinning with the sheer joy of giving.

We then picked up a family video, two great books, and the Christmas dinner: a fat turkey, all the trimmings, dessert, and candy for the boys' stockings. We couldn't wait to deliver our packages.

We do the best we can and leave the rest to the invisible souls who walk beside us.

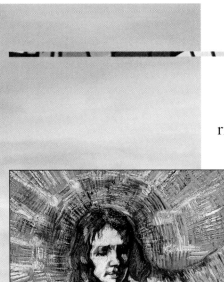

Our cart overflowing, we headed for the checkout line. At first worried about spending too much, I was now filled with a sense of peace. As blessed as we were, we ought to share those blessings with others. Standing in line, the thought kept coming to me that money would be a much-appreciated gift. Maybe there was something this family needed that I didn't know about. Next to the counter were store gift cards on a rack. I looked at the amounts and said a quick prayer for guidance. I reached for the $50 card, but my hand picked up the $100 card. Praying again, I knew this was right, and I laid it on top of my purchases. I made a quick call to my husband to make sure this was not too much, and he surprised me with his assurance to go ahead.

I looked at Nicholas as his eyes fell on the gift card, and I laughed as he wheeled around in shock. "Is that for them?" he asked me. I nodded, and my eyes filled with tears as he threw his arms around me and thanked me. What an amazing kid I have.

That night, we wrapped the presents and delivered the huge box to the Williams' family doorstep. Nick rang the bell, and then we all ran giggling down the street. The feeling of joy stayed with us long past that night. And it returned the day school resumed. Nick ran all the way home from school to tell me Derek and Chad wore their new clothes to school. They fit, and, boy, did they look cool!

The planning and executing of our Secret Santa was the greatest gift our family got that Christmas, and I saw a side to my son that would make any mother weep.

Teenage angels are hard to find these days.

Blossoms for Belle

Meg glanced out the window when she heard the screen door creak next door. She saw Belle heading toward the circus-bright blossoms nodding in her pampered flowerbeds. "Aunt" Belle, Meg reminded herself, even though she was learning that the older woman was no one's aunt, in particular, but claimed as such, in general, by everyone in this new neighborhood. Especially the kids. It was obvious they all adored her.

Speaking of kids . . . Meg sighed. She needed to apologize for the way her own had acted. *What an embarrassing first introduction to a neighbor.* She headed out the door.

"Are your flowers this abundant every year?" Meg frowned at the dandelions freckling her own back lawn.

"Oh, my, yes." Aunt Belle plucked a spindly weed and pinched a spent bloom. "They are my pride and joy."

"I can see that. You spend a great deal of time working with them, and it shows. Your yard is beautiful! Obviously, my kids think so, too," Meg rushed to add. "I'm sorry my daughter picked your new bedding petunias, Belle. It won't happen again."

"Don't let it worry you, dear. Children are more important than flowers. I can always plant more; they'll come back." Aunt Belle adjusted her faded and frayed straw hat.

But it did worry Meg. As the weeks wore on, her kids quickly made new friends up and down the block. Now an entire army of children stormed the house and yard in summertime abandon. No matter how much she cautioned—and threatened—they overflowed into the yard next door. Meg paid another visit to Aunt Belle.

"I noticed that our basketball knocked the blossoms off your prized peonies. I'm so sorry."

It didn't seem to frazzle Aunt Belle. As the weeks wore on, her yard took a backseat when it came to the kids. In fact, she championed them, all the while encouraging their visits, laughing at their antics, plying them with homegrown nosegays and homemade treats.

One hot month melted into another. Meg's temper got shorter while her apologies grew longer.

"I see the kids have worn a path through the corner of your lawn. It's their latest 'shortcut.' I can't believe I didn't catch them at it sooner."

"I'm sorry, Aunt Belle. I saw tracks crisscrossing your violets, and I'm personally acquainted with the guilty party. I'll remind him to keep his bicycle on the sidewalk where it belongs."

"Sorry again. Honestly, you must be a saint to put up with all these kids tearing through your beautiful yard. What were they thinking to let the dog roll and dig in your marigold bed? Your beautiful flowers are ruined!"

But, no matter what, Aunt Belle's angelic smile never wavered and neither did her reply. "It's fine, dear. Don't worry so. Children are more important than flowers. They'll come back."

Meg tried not to worry. After all, the children didn't seem to.

They knew Aunt Belle was as quick to forgive as she was to forget. Her broom swept aside their youthful capers right along with the fallen rose petals. And she was as readily available to listen to both sides of a disagreement or to kiss a skinned elbow as she was to praise a winning slam-dunk. Aunt Belle, a born nurturer, became the guardian angel of both her flowers and the blossoming children.

And so the summer passed, as did many summers after that one. The pattern never changed: While her offspring tromped through flowerbeds, Meg begged pardon for more "problems," and Aunt Belle serenely nursed bruised buds. By ones and by twos, all the kids grew up.

Meg grinned as she walked into Room 33 at Four Seasons Manor. There sat her elderly friend—parked in a wheelchair, puttering with a row of posies.

"I can tell that it's summertime again, Aunt Belle, just by glancing at your windowsill. Why, look at all the flowers!"

A dazzling collection lined up in front of the sparkling glass pane. Vases of fresh-cut roses and peonies—flanked by crocks of marigolds and jars of pansies—haloed Aunt Belle's angel-white hair. Her delicate fingers tamped the rich, damp soil that molded a pot of nodding violets.

"Yes, aren't they lovely, dear?" Aunt Belle glowed. "I've had so many visitors lately, mostly children from the old neighborhood. My, my, how they've grown. And each one who visits brings me flowers." Crystal tears flooded her delphinium blue eyes. "What a beautiful surprise!"

Inhaling the earthy, garden blend of fragrance and friend, Meg slipped an arm around fragile shoulders.

"Why, that shouldn't surprise you, Aunt Belle. Don't you remember? You always promised, 'They'll come back.' And you were right. They have."

To believe in angels is to celebrate a
reality you cannot see,
to respect a realm you're not yet ready for.

The Beholder's Eye

Shoving the vacuum into its stall in the hall closet, I stifled a groan. A half-day of housework behind me and I still wasn't ready for the out-of-state company expected any minute. My four small cyclones whirled through, leaving a wake of toys, crumbs, and stray shoes scattered across the recently trackless carpet.

And then I saw them: the sliding doors of the family room that opened onto the patio. The very doors I had washed and scrubbed earlier that morning. Now generous finger streaks and tiny nose prints daubed the freshly polished glass panes.

"And that looks like...." Frowning, I stepped nearer and bent for a closer inspection. "It is! Peanut butter and chocolate cookies smudged all over. Those kids! It's impossible to get this house clean."

Near tears, I plopped onto the couch and grabbed the jangling phone. "Hello?" I growled.

"Hello, dear," answered my mother, a state away. "Are you busy?"

"Oh, you have no idea! We're expecting guests, and I just can't seem to get all the housework caught up around here, and the kids..."

"That reminds me," she interrupted. "I should do some of my own. Housework, that is."

"You? Huh! You have no comprehension of what a dirty house even looks like," I whined. "After all, there's only the two of you. What can there possibly be to clean?"

"Welllll," she drawled with a smile in her voice, "the mirror above the couch is smeared. But you know, dear, every time I look at the sweet baby prints your little ones left there last month, I can't bring myself to wipe them away. After all, I'm still showing off those precious kisses and streaks as priceless artwork to my friends!"

I caught my breath at the perfect timing of the messenger and her message. Oh, Mother understood—with both her remembering heart and her heaven-sent perspective. With her duo status as mother and grandmother, she could look back *and* beyond. And now she had shouldered a new role: angel—winging her way in the nick of time to remind me what was really important.

My gaze careened around the room. A half-eaten cracker here, wadded socks there, tilting towers of picture books in the corner. With four tracks of miniature footprints framing it all.

And crowning the whole mess was a hand-painted masterpiece on the patio doors. Unnumbered. One-of-a-kind. I grinned.

My own piece of priceless artwork.

Angels by the Dozen

obin's finger traced the newborn's delicate eyebrows. First one, then the other. Butterfly kisses hovered over a velvety cheek, flitted against a tiny ear, then lingered at the dimpled chin.

"Are you hungry, little one?" She smoothed the fluffy pink blanket around the sweet baby girl and whispered, "We'll let your mama rest a little longer."

Robin sighed.

Once upon a time she had cuddled another infant. Only then the blanket was blue and the baby her own.

Of course, that was back when all she ever wanted to do was grow up to be a nurse, get married, and have babies... at least a dozen little angels or so. How quickly those hopes had shattered. She thought back to that time, 25 years ago in the spring of her junior year of high school.

"Robin, we need to talk." Mother looked serious, "Now."

They walked into the bedroom and sat on the bed, side-by-side and stiff. Mother knew.

"You're pregnant, aren't you?" Only it sounded less like a question and more like a moan.

Trembling, Robin nodded.

Oddly, her worst fear wasn't the shame of teenage pregnancy. It was confronting her parents' hurt and disappointment. Oh, how she had dreaded the moment of reckoning.

Her parents surprised her. Instead of accusations and anger, they offered their unconditional love. They accepted and supported her. They championed her decision to keep the baby. Not that it was easy.

There was grief for loss of innocence, loss of childhood, and splintered dreams.

There were fights. Over money for toddler togs and toys. Over rules and control and responsibility.

There were the disappointments of public humiliation and personal rejection.

And there was exhaustion. Always trying to make up time lost from school and sleep lost during nighttime feedings.

She remembered one morning in particular. Her baby stirred, but Robin didn't fully awaken until the whimpering started. She squinted at the clock on the nightstand. It couldn't be 2:00 A.M. already! Maybe if she ignored him this time, he would go back to sleep.

"Waahh," her tiny son cried.

She pulled the quilt around her ears.

"Waahh, waahh!"

"Robin," her mother whispered from the doorway. "Robin, your son needs you."

She kept her breathing even and her eyes closed.

"Robin," a little louder.

"Robin," a little more urgently. Her mother sighed, walked into the room, and leaned over the crib.

270

"Are you hungry little fellow?" her mother crooned, lifting the swaddled infant. "We'll let your mama sleep this time."

Robin snuggled deeper into her toasty cocoon.

"Thank you, mama," she sighed and nestled deeper into her pillow.

Oh, there had been mistakes. Some were hers; some were her parents'. After all, this was unchartered territory for each of them, and they simply had to bumble their way through it.

Yet, somehow, they had weathered it together.

She smiled when she recalled her parents' unflagging encouragement and guidance. Only with their help did she finally graduate from high school, certify as a nursing assistant, and successfully single-parent her precious son.

Back from her reveries, Robin walked into her modest living room. At the couch, she paused and leaned down. Her fingers feathered the young mother's scraggly bangs and her gentle kiss brushed a flushed cheek.

Yes, let the new mommy get a few more hours of sleep. Robin would take over this feeding.

She tucked the afghan around the exhausted girl.

Over the years, Robin's couch had pillowed a number of other troubled pregnant teenagers. Like this girl, they, too, lacked the supportive parents that had blessed Robin's life.

Providentially, their paths led directly to her.

With the mantle of Robin's own teen experiences now resting comfortably on her shoulders, she could be there for other unwed mothers. Robin buffered their pain, mediated their family arguments, and praised

We are most like angels when we stand ready to serve the good inside of us.

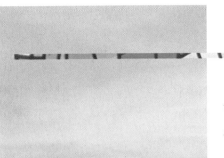

their successes. She hoped they felt the same complete acceptance, safety, and love that Robin's parents once gave her.

"Robin, you're a good little mother."

"Robin, we're proud of you."

"Robin, you're not a bad person. You're a good person who simply made a mistake."

No matter how daunting these teenagers' own mistakes, they had Robin to help them weather the problems. The girls affectionately called her "Mother Angel." They told Robin she was heaven-sent. They told her that they admired her serenity in the face of their heartbreak. That they respected her success and personal example. That they loved her devotion to them. Most importantly, they thanked Robin for restoring their egos and nurturing their fragile dreams.

Robin smiled. After all, some dreams do come true, and she was living proof.

No, she had never married; but she did grow up to become a nurse and raise her son.

No, she hadn't birthed more babies, but she did have children. Lots of children. Even though they arrived half-grown and stayed only a short while—still, they came... at least a dozen or so.

But, an angel? Her? Robin grinned. The way she saw it, these young mothers and their babies were the blessings of her life. They gave her purpose and direction. They made her whole.

They were *her* angels. Each and every one.

Inside and Out

"Gramps, why do you work so hard out here?" Matthew lounged against a weather-rough picket fence, careful not to snag his sleeve on the thorns of his grandfather's old-fashioned climbing roses. He swiped at the sweat beading his brow in the shimmery heat. "You're old, you should be sitting in front of the television sipping lemonade."

The old man smiled and wielded his hoe comfortably, competently. Chocolate-rich soil, moist and mealy, appeared with each gentle churn. Though the worn wooden handle was darkened by years of use, its shiny blade—oiled and rust-free—mirrored the pastel palette of the pampered dahlias waving over it.

"Why are you out here in the flowerbeds when you could be napping?" Matthew plucked a pink earthworm from a crumbling clod. "Grandma says some people have guardian angels but that you're her garden angel. Is that why, Gramps? Because you're always working here among her flowers?" He rolled the stretchy worm like clay against his palm.

Rescuing the thinning night crawler from an uncertain future, Matthew's grandfather tucked it under a clump of fleecy-leafed foxglove and looked up at the boy.

"Well, you know Matthew, for 52 years now Grandma has been the angel of my heart. She fills my life with joy and our house with fresh-cut flowers." Gramps caressed the petals of a velvety pansy. "Oh, how she loves bringing springtime indoors. So, Matthew, some time ago I decided that it was MY job to do whatever it takes outside to bring a little springtime inside to your grandmother's heart."

Gramps surveyed the garden with a satisfied smile. "Garden angel, huh? Well, maybe. You see, I help God provide the flowers!"

Created beings, we are all made,
angels and babies alike. We are created, loved,
and filled with the wonder of discovery.

274

All Is Bright

You know how some Christmases are etched in your memory? How you recall them in vivid detail? For me, it's the Christmas of 1978. Or, rather, the week prior to that holiday.

Baking seasonal treats to deliver to neighbors was a tradition in our family. It was also as much of an exercise in organization as it was a lesson in cooperation when Mother marshaled all eight of us children into the kitchen one December evening.

"Bessie, I'm putting you in charge of both the cookie batter and the twins. Here is the recipe. Here are the twins."

"Ruth, I think you can manage to find and gather sprinkles, red hots, and chocolate chips to decorate with."

"Boys, come with me, and I'll teach you the art of making your Granny's special frosting."

As the six-year-old family caboose, I was dubbed "Jill-of-all-trades" and ended up being the official helper. Everyone's helper. Oh, how I loved helping.

I helped Bessie and the twins.

"I know Daddy likes crispy cookies, but get those eggshells out of my batter!" demanded Bessie.

I helped Ruth.

"Absolutely no rubber-band halos on these cookies," Ruth insisted.

I helped Mother and the boys.

"No, I don't think eight cups of sugar is better than two," said Mother.

As you might imagine, mixing, cutting, baking, and icing took us well into the night. In spite of all I did to help.

Finally, all the mixing bowls, spoons, and baking sheets (trust me, we used a lot of them) had been washed and put away. All the flat surfaces (and, yes, that included the floor) had been wiped clean of spills. All the cookies had been cut and decorated (with a serious attention to detail genetically programmed into each of us) and set aside. Mother dug out her giant plastic bowls.

Gingerly, each sweet treat was lifted. Proudly, each work of art was admired. Not a star was chipped, not a halo cracked. After we filled and stacked three huge containers, I grabbed the last lid and stretched all the way across the counter to help...and bumped my elbow.

Down came the pile—bowls, cookies, and all.

Talk about "Silent Night." We all stared at the floor. Then everybody looked at me. No one said a word—at least for a minute. Which was exactly enough time for me to race to my bedroom and bury my head under a pillow.

Then, through my sobs, I heard her: Mother crooning as she rubbed my back. At last I quieted enough to listen. Only, I didn't hear the lecture that I deserved and expected from my tired, disappointed parent.

"Don't cry," she said. "They're just cookies."

Gathering me in her arms, Mother tucked my head under her chin and began to hum as she rocked me. Then she started to chuckle.

That couldn't be. Suspiciously, I pulled back and looked up—right into her smiling face.

"Are you *laughing?*"

"Yes," said Mother. "I certainly am. After all, in 25 years we'll laugh about this, so why wait? Why don't you and I go ahead and laugh now?"

"*Now?*"

"Now."

I smiled through my tears. And I vividly remember how they made a shiny, shimmery halo around my mother's head.

A lot of Christmases have come and gone since then. So many, in fact, that this Christmas I'll follow family tradition and make holiday cookies with my own little helper. But the memory of that particular Christmas doesn't dim with time. It only gets brighter. You could even say it glows.

Always listen for an angel's voice;
you'll speak more gently yourself.

Full Circle

She was there when I breathed my first breath, and I was there when she breathed her last: my mother.

Once she discovered her kidneys were failing, Mom ignored the complaints of her rheumatoid joints and got herself to a New Jersey clinic for weekly dialysis. All the while she continued to be the shoulder her neighborhood leaned on. As far back as I can remember, she had a bandage for everything from playground cuts and scrapes to emotional lumps and bumps. She always had the coffee on, an extra potato in the pot, or a nice, cool drink waiting for anyone who showed up—and people did. I can hardly recall a dinner with just the four of us, and no matter the guest, our after-dinner conversation often digressed into raucous discussions involving politics or religion. Mom sat knitting, soaking it all in, and when things got too hot she'd say, "Now, now," and whip out the warm apple cobbler to tone us all down.

Mom did hospice in a time when neighborhoods and families were breaking down. Grown children didn't stay to care for their parents anymore but moved across country to pursue "opportunity." When people asked Mom why she spent her time absorbing the tears of others, she'd shrug in her pragmatic way and say, "We've all got to look after each other. Each other is all we've got."

From my home in Pennsylvania, I pictured her stepping off the bus in front of the dialysis clinic: silver hair freshly combed, her standard floral blouse buttoned high worn over navy or black slacks, handbag securely hooked over a bent elbow, and, finally, rubber-soled ground grippers—practical shoes—not the open-toed variety with heels and ankle straps that were her trademark in her younger years o. She gave the impression she was there to visit a patient not be one. So I never imagined the day my "Lady Bug," the gracious woman who always flew home to care for her children, friends, and neighbors, might need help. But here she was on the other end of the phone saying, "Ooh, I hurt."

So I drove down to Jersey to be with Mom. She had lost so much strength, but her mind still honed in on humor and politics and keeping tabs on what she could. What seemed to upset her most about her illness wasn't so much the pain or the inconvenience of housing a bright soul in a failing body, it was the winding down, becoming the one who needed care as opposed to the one who gave it.

After I'd been with Mom a few days, I found her doubled into herself in the middle of the night, conscious but barely coherent except for her refrain of, "Ooh, I hurt." We cabbed to the emergency entrance at Overlook Hospital despite her garbled protest that we should use the main door like everyone else. The doctor on duty admitted her, and the next morning her own doctor said the dialysis wasn't going well, that they'd have to go to the next step: peritoneal dialysis.

If angels had a job description, it would only consist of one task: Do the work of love.

By this time the family had assembled. My brother, Kenneth, and his wife and sons; my fiancé, Michael; my daughter, Stacey, and her fiancé; and my son were all gathered around Lady Bug's bed listening as the doctor explained that peritoneal dialysis wasn't a step to healing but only a prolonging of the end. Hooked up to an array of machines, Mom drifted in and out of consciousness.

I bent over her, took her hand, and her eyes fluttered open. "Mom," I asked, "do you want to go home?"

A slight nod.

"Do you understand if you go home, it's to die?"

Her arms stretched to me and, in a whisper, she said, "Take me home."

"Good enough for me."

The rest of the family nodded in agreement. On my way out of her room to secure an ambulance for the ride home, I bumped into a tall man in black and noticed the white collar. "Are you a priest?" I asked as I held on to his arm.

He glanced at my hand. "Why, yes, I am."

"Good, we need you in here. My Mom needs the anointing of the sick. We're taking her home to die."

His round eyes opened wider and he covered my hand with his. "This is marvelous," he said. "It usually doesn't happen this way." Within the hour we were on our way back to the home Mom and Dad built many years earlier, the one she'd lived in all her married life.

Mom's tiny home filled with family. It was Friday night, and we all decided to camp out and take turns keeping vigil. For the next day and a half, we rotated in and out of her room, always someone at her side. During my turn, I kept nodding off in the chair. So I decided to slip in bed next to Mom. I curled up to her back, and put my arm around her, thinking I'd just rest a few minutes. But I fell into a deep sleep. I dreamt I was weightless, breathing clean air, every cell in my body vibrating and every sense exploding as I sped along a bright white tunnel.

I'd never been to a place like this before, and I wanted to find out where it was so I could come back and bring all my family and friends with me. I woke from the dream in a gasp for breath. I was fully awake and still energized, but something had changed. My focus went to my arm draped over Mom. There was no rise and fall, no breath from her body. I sat up and took her pulse; I realized that what woke me was the rattle of her last breath. Her last breath took my breath away.

Mom gave me this incredible gift. In life she was my anchor, and in death she took me with her as far as I could go. As much as I wanted to, I couldn't follow her because it wasn't my time yet. Lady Bug took care of me by letting me know the place she was going was safe and good. She didn't want me to cry but to feel the joy of that place, to have my tears dry by morning. Mom died with a smile on her soul, and she wanted me to smile when I thought of her. Before going out to tell the rest of the family, I kissed her cheek and whispered in her ear, "Thanks, Mom. Say hi to Dad for me."

No one can ever tell me there's no such thing as an angel.

A Friend in Need

My sweaty hands gripped the steering wheel as I jerked the car into the far right lane. I peered ahead at the merge ramp getting closer. Monday morning commuters swelled the surface street, and I knew it would be even worse on the freeway.

Oh, God, I'm so scared. The interstate is too crowded, the traffic too fast, the noise too loud.

What was I doing, navigating rush hour in L.A.? It felt worse than driving down the wrong side of the road in a foreign country. And I was such an inexperienced driver that I rarely attempted highway travel at home. My nose twitched at the fumes—diesel, motor oil, and rubber.

Dear God, even this loaner car I'm using feels alien.

The driver ahead of me hit his brakes, and so did I. My heart slammed in my chest. A horn honked. At me? I jerked my head around—first left, then right—checking to see what I had done wrong.

Cars whizzed by. A rumbling tractor-trailer boxed me in.

Please just give me courage. Please keep me safe.

Los Angeles loomed ahead like a concrete jungle. I heard the noise; I felt the confusion; I sensed the danger. It was a far cry from my safe little Colorado town nestled against the foothills of the Rockies. The home I'd left behind weeks earlier.

Flipping the turn signal, I gradually nosed the small car into another lane. Again a horn honked. My head pivoted. At me?

Although the gas gauge in the car registered full, I knew that I was running on empty. Not sleeping. Not eating. Spending so many weeks bedside in the Trauma Unit with my comatose son was taking its toll. Being far from home, on my own, and alone, seemed to magnify the stress. Somehow I needed to change gears, refuel, find some serenity amidst all this chaos.

The tangled traffic slowed and belly-crawled along, nose to rump. A semi snarled; a truck growled; a low-slung sports car snapped at my tail.

Taking advantage of the change in pace, I shoved in a cassette I had received in the mail the day before. I turned the black knob and heard—a friend, a dear friend. A welcome voice from home. It was Sue, reminding me to have faith. Sue, encouraging me to be strong. Sue, prodding me to rely on God. She ended the tape with an old story.

A story about the king who offered a reward for a painting that portrayed perfect peace.

Eager artists scattered throughout his kingdom in search of the model setting, the ideal subject—the paragon of peace. They looked high; they looked low. They sketched; they painted. And they brought their best efforts for the royal consideration of the king.

As the pictures were presented, each received the king's undivided attention. Sorting, sifting, and tossing them aside, he bestowed his approval on only two.

The first painting portrayed a placid, blue lake that mirrored billowing clouds, rolling hills, and tranquil, towering mountains.

The royal court murmured in assent. Indeed, this was the perfect picture of peace.

The second painting also revealed mountains—jagged and stony. An angry sky, split by lightning, spitting rain into a plunging waterfall.

The royal court rumbled, surprised that this painting, too, found favor with the king.

But he pointed out details they had missed.

"Peer closely—through the waterfall," the king ordered.

The royal court crowded closer.

"Observe the fragile bush growing in a crack in the rock."

The royal court leaned forward.

"See the delicate bird sitting, untroubled, on her nest."

The royal court squinted its eyes.

"It is this painting that wins the award. I so decree!"

The royal court gasped.

"How can that be?" they all murmured.

"Because," answered the king, "this artist made a profound discovery. He learned that peace is not a place without noise, confusion, or fear. He learned that peace means being in the midst of all those things and remaining calm in your heart."

Being in the midst of all those things . . .

It was just like Sue to know exactly how to help me. She was an angel at my side. An angel in my greatest time of need. Because of Sue, I knew then what I needed most: to sit quietly and listen to the "still small voice" of God.

I needed to remain calm in my heart. I needed to find peace within because I certainly would find no peace without.

I exited the highway. A horn honked. My head swiveled.

At me?

Surprise Package

Pamela Martin and her fellow fifth-graders were appalled when their teacher, Miss Roberts, told them that a nearby nursing home had only one old television. The picture was snowy and tended to blank out altogether in the middle of the residents' favorite programs.

Miss Roberts suggested that raising money for a new television—about $300—would make a good class project for Christmas. That sum didn't seem like so much to Pamela. She suggested a raffle; someone else wanted to hold a bake sale. A father donated a computer from his office to be used as a prize in the raffle, and the kids sold chances door-to-door at a $1 each. The children worked so hard they thought they surely had raised more than enough money. The class let out a collective groan when Pamela announced the total: $150.

After long hours of baking, then a week of selling cookies and brownies after school, the class earned another $50. They were still $100 short.

Earning money for the TV wouldn't be as easy as they had thought, the children realized, and they might not have enough by Christmas. As pressed as she was to make ends meet on her salary, Miss Roberts even considered writing a check to make up the difference, but she then decided the children probably needed to accomplish this on their own.

Pamela usually arrived early at school because her mother dropped her off on the way to work. One day she started up the steps and, about halfway up, almost tripped over a square metal box. She tried to lift it and open it. It was too heavy for a little girl, and a combination lock secured the lid. She went in and found Miss Roberts, who lifted the box and carried it into the classroom, where it sat until the rest of the children arrived. Everyone took turns guessing what could be inside. Half joking, one boy said, "Maybe it's a bomb!"

Miss Roberts realized he could be right. She picked up the phone to call the principal. The fire alarm sounded, and the children filed outside.

Then fire trucks and police cars roared up, sirens screaming. A TV crew showed up and started filming as a firefighter carefully carried out the box and hauled it away. A short time later, a police officer returned the box with the lock cut away. The principal carried it to Miss Roberts.

"You guys might like to see this," he said, smiling.

When Miss Roberts opened the lid, the contents gleamed dully. Coins! The box was full of quarters. Miss Roberts unfolded the note taped to the inside top of the box lid and read the words aloud: "I heard about your project to buy a TV for the nursing home. I have been saving coins for years, and this seems like a good way to use them."

The note was signed, "A friend." But the kids called the mysterious giver their TV angel!

Trust your angels to guide your steps.
Trust your feet to take them.